# Heart Healthy Cookbook for Beginners

*1000-Day Delicious Recipes for Low-Sodium, Low-Fat Meals to Improve Your Health and Lower Your Blood Pressure*

Tryna Pany

# Table of Contents

# Introduction

Heart health is very important in one's life. And because of our lifestyle and eating habits, heart disease has become rampant in modern times. Fortunately, your heart health is in your hands, and there's something you can do to ensure your health and longevity. For example, through diet, but before you eat, you have to take the time to understand the foods you want to eat, because they will determine the life span of your heart function. However, with this Heart Healthy Cookbook, you will be able to see a new direction and make the right choice. A healthy diet is the best weapon against any heart disease. You will learn about different aspects of nutrition as well as healthy lifestyle, which will help you avoid any challenges that are often characteristic of an unhealthy lifestyle and eating habits.

Let't start!

# Chapter 1: Eating Heart-Healthy Made Easy

Welcome to heart-healthy eating! This chapter lays out the nuts and bolts of eating heart-healthy and provides the info and tools to do so easily. It also covers some frequently asked questions; touches on some common heart medications and food interactions; provides a list of fresh, frozen, and pantry essentials; and offers shopping shortcuts and meal-planning tips. You'll learn how to make quick and flavorful heart-healthy food without added salt and fat.

## Love Your Heart Through Food

Everyone is at a different stage of their heart-health journey. Some of you may have an official diagnosis, some may be recovering from cardiac surgery, and others might use this as a preventative measure.

Nutrition is the most powerful tactic you can utilize to heal your body and protect your heart. There are certain foods that can negatively contribute to heart disease and clog your arteries, causing restriction of blood flow and narrowing of blood vessels. These foods are high in trans-fat, which is primarily found in fried foods and hydrogenated oils; saturated fat, which is primarily found in meats like beef, pork, and lamb; processed meats like hot dogs, salami, and sausages; and high-fat dairy products like cheese, butter, whole milk, and ghee. However, there are many foods that are needed for your body and heart to function properly and improve blood flow and blood vessel health.

Heart-healthy foods include rich sources of antioxidants and polyphenols that protect the heart against harmful stresses (such as quercetin in fennel and anthocyanins in red cabbage and berries), nitric oxide-containing foods that increase blood flow (such as arugula, kale, garlic, sesame seeds, and pumpkin seeds), omega-3-rich foods that fight inflammation (such as salmon and sardines), B vitamin-rich foods that help stabilize plaque formation (such as chickpeas, lean chicken breast, and edamame), fiber-rich foods that help promote proper excretion of excess cholesterol from the body (such as whole grains, fruits, and vegetables), fresh herbs and spices that reduce swelling (such as turmeric and garlic), and magnesium and potassium-rich foods that help maintain a proper heartbeat, heart function, and blood pressure (such as avocados, lentils, and dark chocolate).

I understand that any kind of diet and lifestyle change isn't easy, but I am here to help smooth the way by providing clear instructions and delicious examples.

## Caring For A Loved One

I can empathize with the gravity of caring for someone with heart disease. Managing that and your own life may feel like a huge task. So, here are five tips for caregivers to make things a bit easier:

- Make one meal for everyone

If you make one meal for the whole family, you'll free up a lot of your time and reduce stress. If others really want to add more salt, they can adjust on their own.

- Go to the grocery store prepared

Try discussing two to four meals to make for the week. Involving your loved one in the process allows them to feel heard, which can help encourage them to eat the meals. Write out the days of the week, the meals planned for each, and the groceries needed.

- Make leftovers your friend

Pick one or two days to meal prep. Double the recipe of a particular dish your loved one enjoys most and freeze it in individual portions so they can easily thaw and warm it up as needed. Consider preassembling smoothie or meal ingredients and sauces to make meal prep even quicker.

- Be supportive, even if they eat something they're "not supposed to."

You don't want them to hide things from you. Ask if there is a way you can make a healthier version more appealing. You can ask them what flavor profile they are in the mood for, and then you can easily add that flavor element to a snack or meal. By listening to them and their preferences, they feel supported in their journey.

- Have a favorite seasoning blend.

Make a go-to seasoning blend, so that when you're in a pinch, they can add flavor to their own food by using a dash of the salt-free spice blend.

# What Does a Heart-Healthy Diet Look Like?

In this section, we'll address the popular and well- documented heart-healthy diets and the common questions people have about eating heart-healthy.

## Mediterranean, Dash, And Plant-Based Diets

Although there isn't one best heart-healthy diet, many prominent medical establishments, including the American College of Cardiology, generally agree that plant-based diets such as the Mediterranean, DASH (Dietary Approaches to Stop Hypertension), and vegetarian diets are the heart-healthiest ways to eat. This book's recipes all comply with at least one of these three diets.

Plant-based diets are heart-healthy because they significantly reduce the consumption of many animal products that are high in artery- clogging saturated fat and trimethylamine N-oxide derivatives, such as red meat. Plant-based diets are also cardio-protective because the foods abundantly recommended contain heart-healthy vitamins, minerals, fiber, polyunsaturated fats, and anti-inflammatory antioxidants.

Plant-based diets emphasize plant foods, while de-emphasizing some animal products. A vegetarian diet removes meat and sometimes fish, dairy, and eggs. The Mediterranean and DASH diets are rich in vegetables, fruits, nuts, beans, seeds, whole grains, low-fat or nonfat dairy, and have moderate amounts of fish and poultry. The Mediterranean diet emphasizes red wine consumption and monounsaturated fats (such as olive oil), while the DASH diet emphasizes sodium reduction.

The DASH diet protects the heart by helping lower blood pressure in individuals with high blood pressure, along with reducing bad LDL cholesterol and improving insulin resistance. High blood pressure means too much pressure is placed on the blood vessel walls, leading to stressed, overworked arteries that can scar and be more susceptible to plaque buildup-increasing the risk of blood clots, stroke, and heart disease. This diet emphasizes sodium reduction along with an increase in potassium, magnesium, and calcium for optimal blood vessel health.

The Mediterranean diet mirrors the DASH diet and emphasizes consuming moderate amounts of monounsaturated fat from extra-virgin olive oil, avocados, and certain nuts. In the PREDIMED study, the diet's extra heart-healthy monounsaturated fat reduced the risk of cardiovascular events by about 30 percent compared to a low-fat diet. Replacing saturated fat with monounsaturated fat also significantly decreases LDL and triglyceride levels-if either parameter is elevated, it can increase the risk of a stroke or heart attack.

## What About Low-Carb Diets?

Low-carbohydrate diets, specifically the ketogenic and paleo diets, replace carbohydrates with fat and therefore are not optimal heart-healthy diets. The ketogenic diet can restrict carbohydrates to 20 to 50 grams per day, which is dangerously low for optimal brain and heart function. The National Academy of Medicine established a recommended daily intake of at least 130 grams per day for adults to achieve the needed amount of glucose for the brain to function properly. Additionally, these diets can contain up to 70 to 80 percent total calories from fat, with a large quantity of artery-clogging saturated fat. Low-carbohydrate diets can also place you at risk for deficiencies of vitamins and minerals such as potassium, magnesium, folate, biotin, thiamin, selenium, and vitamins A and E.

## What If I Have A Crossover Condition?

Many individuals dealing with heart disease may also have another condition that can further impact the way they eat. For instance, some may have prediabetes, diabetes, or insulin resistance, and should also focus on carbohydrate type and amount, along with dietary fiber. Others may have varying stages of chronic kidney disease and may have to focus on their individual needs for protein, potassium, phosphorus, and fluid consumption to avoid overtaxing their kidneys. For those managing their weight, I would recommend to particularly home in on hunger and satiety cues before and after meal consumption. Meeting one on one with a registered dietitian can help individuals achieve optimal results by simultaneously addressing an individual's chronic conditions, lifestyle factors, and food preferences.

## What If I Am Recovering From Heart Surgery?

Cardiac surgery has been shown to create a cascade of inflammatory responses, which can lead to more complications, such as multiple-organ injury and dysfunction. Adequate and balanced post- surgery nutrition is important for various reasons, including reducing postoperative complications and improving wound healing. Specific, well-researched studies show that protein, vitamins D and C, and selenium are stressed as being integral components of an optimal post-surgery diet. If you don't have an appetite and cannot eat large meals, consume small meals more frequently to obtain all the necessary nutrients to protect your heart and promote functional recovery and healing.

## Heart Medications And Food Interactions

If you're taking medication, there are some food- drug interactions to be aware of. Talk to your doctor about any medications you're taking and potential dietary changes.

- Statins with Grapefruit or Pomegranate

Grapefruit has a high concentration of furanocoumarins, which are plant-based compounds that block the enzyme needed to break down specific statins (a class of drugs that lower cholesterol levels) and calcium channel blockers (a class of blood pressure medications). Grapefruit may increase blood levels of a statin by 8 to 260 percent and may reduce calcium channel blocker effectiveness by about half. Furanocoumarins are also found in pomegranates and may have the same effect.

- Coumadin (Warfarin) and Vitamin K

Oftentimes vitamin Kis looked at as a vitamin to avoid if you are taking Coumadin, a blood-thinning medication; I want to debunk this myth. First, vitamin K is needed in blood clotting when a blood vessel is injured, and a deficiency can increase the risk of excess bleeding. A deficiency can also cause an increase in calcium buildup in the heart because vitamin Kis needed to efficiently place calcium in the bones.

Coumadin reduces blot clotting by blocking vitamin K-dependent blood-clotting factors. Your blood's ability to clot is closely monitored by testing your clotting time, also known as your international normalized ratio (INR) lab test. The doctor will adjust your Coumadin dosage to keep your INR within a target range. Therefore, vitamin Kintake needs to be consistent for the Coumadin dosage to be tightly regulated, and a sudden change is not advised. In addition, consuming high-dose supplements of garlic, turmeric, ginkgo biloba, St. John's wort, vitamin E, and/or omega-3 fatty acids with blood-thinning medications can be dangerous. Taking these supplements together with these medications can thin your blood to extremely dangerous levels and may increase your risk of internal bleeding.

## The Heart of the Heart-Healthy Diet

A heart-healthy diet's essence is balance: lean protein, heart-healthy fats, and complex carbohydrates. The goal is to decrease the consumption of artery-clogging foods and add nutrient-rich cardioprotective foods that are plentiful in vitamins, minerals, and antioxidants. Here are a few guiding principles:

- Eat lean protein

Lean protein includes legumes, beans, egg whites, omega-3-rich fish, low-fat dairy, and chicken breast. Adding in more nonprocessed, plant-based options is an easy way to actively reduce inflammation. Lean protein also adds a host of cardioprotective vitamins and minerals, such as potassium, magnesium, selenium, and vitamin B6.

- Choose unsaturated fat over saturated fat

Prioritizing unsaturated fats over trans and saturated ones helps remove bad cholesterol and increase good cholesterol. Unsaturated fats include avocados, avocado oil, olive oil, nuts, seeds, and omega-3-rich fish. Portions need to be monitored because fat has more calories than protein and carbohydrates, but a small portion is encouraged at each meal.

- Pick complex carbs high in dietary fiber

Dietary fiber protects your heart by significantly reducing your total cholesterol and LDL levels. Studies show every additional 7 grams of dietary fiber per day may lower your cardiovascular disease risk by 9 percent. Complex carbohydrates such as vegetables, whole grains, beans, legumes, and fruits contain varying amounts of soluble and insoluble fiber. Soluble fiber traps carbohydrates and bile acids during digestion, and insoluble fiber allows for proper elimination. Both soluble fiber and insoluble fiber work in tandem to reduce blood sugar and lipid levels and keep your arteries clean.

- Prioritize antioxidants

Consuming an antioxidant-rich diet also helps reduce inflammation. Inflammation promotes plaque growth that clogs arteries and may cause blood clots, thereby increasing the risk of heart attacks and strokes. Making dishes that are antioxidant-rich and feature vegetables and high-fiber fruits is an easy way to helplower inflammation in your body.

- Reduce your salt intake

Low-sodium diets are a mainstream recommendation in heart-healthy diets, and they are backed by significant research. While we need to focus on a low-sodium diet, we also need to emphasize the importance of adding in fresh herbs (such as basil and dill), spices (such as oregano and garlic), and flavorful foods (such as onions and leeks) to make foods enjoyable and tasty. Consuming potassium-rich foods, such as cooked spinach, cooked broccoli, and sweet potatoes, helps eliminate excess sodium in your body, which helps lower blood pressure and improve circulation.

- Bake, steam, and roast your way to success

Your meal's preparation can significantly impact your blood pressure and cholesterol management. Swap deep-fried foods for foods that are baked, steamed, roasted, or grilled for a boost in nutrient absorption and optimal blood-vessel health.

- Attune to your hunger cues

Maintaining a healthy metabolic rate and body weight by listening to your body's hunger and satiety cues also lessens the stress on your heart. Consuming food within one hour of waking up and timing food consumption based off your hunger signals is imperative to keeping your metabolism revved through the day and as you age. When you are slightly hungry, you should eat, and when you are slightly satisfied, you should stop.

Consuming a heart-healthy diet can be easily implemented by eating more cardioprotective foods and limiting foods that add stress to your heart and circulatory system. See the following charts for a comprehensive list.

## Foods to Love, Limit, and Let Go

This table looks at different categories of foods to love, limit, and let go of. The "To Love" category represents a better choice for your heart when eaten in moderation as part of a well-balanced meal. Grains should still be limited to 1/3 to 1/2 cup per serving and dairy, fish, poultry, and soy to about 4 to 6 ounces per serving, depending on the individual.

## Shopping Shortcuts and Planning Pro Tips

The first step to cooking heart-healthy is to shop smart and plan ahead. You may no longer be able to rely on some of the shortcuts you took before, such as using high-sodium bottled sauces or ordering takeout if you didn't plan dinner. Here are some ways to make heart-healthy shopping and meal planning easier.

- Plan out the week ahead and have a grocery list

Decide what recipes you'll make for the week and write a grocery list with the items you need. Consider choosing recipes with ingredients that overlap and buying those items in bulk.

- Buy frozen or pre-cut vegetables

To lessen prep time and avoid the extra salt in canned vegetables, buy frozen vegetables or bagged, pre-chopped vegetables instead. Many stores also have vegetables cut into strips, which can make an easy slaw. A report prepared by the Environmental Quality and Food Safety Research Unit at the University of Chester showed that some vegetables, particularly frozen broccoli, carrots, and Brussels sprouts, contained more vitamin C, lutein, and beta-carotene than fresh!

- Have a go-to spice blend

Make a seasoning blend of spices you enjoy and have it on hand to quickly season lean protein without the added sodium. really like savory, so a Mediterranean blend of paprika, cumin, turmeric, and black pepper is a staple in my home. With your favorite spice blend, you can make simple and easy meals by shaking the blend over a protein, vegetables, and a whole grain carbohydrate, and then cooking them in a heart-healthy way.

- Cook in bulk

Double batch and freeze herbs, sauces, or parts of a meal so you can eliminate a step in the cooking process when you are in a pinch for time. For example, cut up a whole bunch of basil and divide it into 1-teaspoon increments in ice cube trays; add water and freeze for easy use. Next time you need it to spice up a dish or make a quick pesto sauce, easily defrost it in the actual pan or overnight in the refrigerator. You can also prep and prepack smoothie ingredients to make a quick breakfast smoothie in the morning.

- Keep pantry staples on hand.

Keep a stock of frozen essentials and pantry staple items such as low-sodium, Tetra Pak canned beans and frozen vegetables. Stocking these staples means you'll have all the ingredients for an easy meal if you don't have time to cook or find that you've forgotten an ingredient that you can easily replace with something else.

- Repurpose leftovers.

If you're having chicken, fish, tofu, or a bean dish for dinner you can take the leftovers and shred them, or just add them to the top of a salad for another meal. If you have leftover salad or vegetables, throw them in a pot with your favorite heart-healthy protein for an easy balanced meal.

## Reading Nutrition Labels

Reading a product's nutritional label is as important as reading its ingredients. A nutritional label is a chart on the back of most packaged foods that details the ingredients and nutritional content of the item. Items to pay close attention to include saturated and trans fats, sodium, carbohydrates, dietary fiber, and added sugar. Saturated fats should be limited to 2 grams or less per serving due to its artery-clogging effect. Avoid trans fats completely because they accelerate atherosclerosis; aim for 0 grams. Check the ingredients list for "hydrogenated oils"; if those are in the list, leave it on the shelf. Limit sodium to 150 milligrams per snack serving and 300 milligrams per meal serving because of its negative arterial effects.

Carbohydrates are necessary because they contribute dietary fiber and essential vitamins and nutrients; however, consume them in moderation to avoid weight gain and minimize plaque formation. First look at the total carbohydrates, it should be between or less than 15 to 20 grams of carbohydrates per serving in a snack or between or less than 30 to 45 grams of carbohydrates in a meal, after accounting for dietary fiber. To account for the dietary fiber, subtract the total grams of carbohydrates from the total grams of fiber. For instance, a slice of bread may contain 20 grams of carbohydrates and 5 grams of dietary fiber; the total net carbohydrates would be 15 grams. Aim for dietary fiber to be at least 4 grams in a whole grain food, such as high-fiber cereals or whole wheat breads.

Added sugars include any sugars that are added to your food during the processing or packaging process, and should be limited as much as possible. The American Heart Association recommends the maximum amount of sugar consumption be about 6 teaspoons (25 grams) per day for women and about 9 teaspoons (37.5 grams) per day for men.

## Find the Easiest Cooking Method for You

This book is easy in three different ways, so you can pick the one that best suits you: 5 ingredients (excluding oil, salt, water, and pepper), meaning less prep; 30-minute meals (or less), meaning a quick cook time; and one-pot, meaning less cleanup. Everyone's idea of easy is different and what may be easy one day may not be easy the next. For instance, on weeknights, you may choose a 30-minute meal, and on weekends, you might prefer a one-pot meal, even if it needs to cook for a little bit longer.

## Effortless Ways To Boost Flavor Without Added Salt And Fat

One of the biggest complaints about heart-healthy foods is that they are flavorless and bland. I have endeavored to ensure that all the recipes are tasty and full of flavor without adding unhealthy fats or salt. One of the ways I boost flavor in some of the recipes is by combining aromatics such as garlic, shallots, ginger, and leeks with fresh herbs in a sauce, such as a Cilantro-Mint Sauce or a pesto sauce, to top a dish. Flavor is also created by blending and marrying

spices to make, for instance, a barbeque flavor or chile-lime flavor, without the added salt. Cooking methods such as broiling, roasting, and pan-searing enable the natural sugars in the vegetables to add a robust flavor. Many times the dish does not need much oil, but rather needs a liquid to cook in; citrus juices, water, broth, or a nut or seed base are used to cut the fat and make a dish delicious. This also allows you to easily mix and match different sauces, proteins, vegetables, and flavors to complement your or your loved one's mood and taste buds. Just be mindful the cooking times may vary depending on the swap.

# Chapter 2: Breakfast

## Whole-Wheat Blueberry Muffins

Quick & easy
Prep time: 5 minutes
Cook time: 23 minutes

### Ingredients:

- Olive oil nonstick cooking spray
- 3/4 cup whole-wheat flour
- 1/2 teaspoon baking soda
- Pinch salt
- 2 teaspoons granulated stevia or 2 tablespoons brown sugar
- 2 egg whites, beaten
- 1/4 cup shredded zucchini
- 3 tablespoons nonfat milk or plant-based milk
- 1/2 teaspoon vanilla extract
- 1/2 cup blueberries (fresh or frozen)

### Method:

1. Preheat the oven to 375°F and lightly spray two cups of a giant muffin pan with the cooking spray.
2. In a large bowl, whisk together the flour, baking soda, salt, and stevia. Set it aside.
3. In a small bowl, stir together the egg whites, zucchini, milk, and vanilla.
4. Stir the wet ingredients into the dry ingredients. Gently fold in the blueberries.
5. Divide the batter equally between the prepared muffin cups. Bake for 19 to 23 minutes, or until a toothpick inserted in the center comes out clean.
6. Let them cool for 3 minutes before enjoying.

### Nutritional Content:

- Calories: 270
- Fats: 1g
- Protein: 11g
- Cholesterol: 0mg
- Carbohydrates: 55g
- Fiber: 3g
- Sodium: 451mg

# Salmon And Avocado Toast

Serves 3
Hands-on time: 15 min
Total time: 15 min

## Ingredients:

- 1½ whole-grain bagels, split
- 1 (7.6-ounce) can sockeye salmon, drained
- 1 tablespoon extra-virgin olive oil
- 1 avocado, peeled and pitted
- 1 tablespoon freshly squeezed lime juice
- 1/2 cup chopped fresh tomatoes
- 1/4 cup minced red onion (optional)
- Freshly ground black pepper (optional)

## Method:

1. Toast the bagels.
2. Meanwhile, in a medium bowl, mix the salmon with the olive oil, breaking up the pieces.
3. In a small bowl, mash the avocado with the lime juice.
4. Top each toasted bagel half with some salmon mix. Spread the avocado on top of the salmon, followed by the tomatoes, then onion and pepper (if using).

## Nutritional Content:

- Calories: 366
- Fats: 18g
- Cholesterol: 47mg
- Sodium: 463mg
- Carbohydrates: 27g
- Fiber: 7g
- Protein: 27g

# Peach-Cranberry Sunrise Muesli

Serves 1
Hands-on time: 5 min
Total time: 15 min

**Ingredients:**

- 1/3 cup vanilla soy milk
- 3 tablespoons rolled oats
- 1 tablespoon chia seeds
- 1 tablespoon buckwheat (optional, see tip)
- 1 peach
- 1 tablespoon dried cranberries
- 1 tablespoon sunflower seeds

**Method:**

1. Mix the soy milk, oats, chia seeds, and buckwheat (if using) in a large bowl. Soak for at least 10 minutes (and as long as overnight).
2. Meanwhile, cut the peach into bite-size pieces.
3. When the oats have softened up, sprinkle with the cranberries, sunflower seeds, and peach chunks.

**Nutritional Content:**

- Calories: 361
- Fats: 11g
- Cholesterol: 0mg
- Sodium: 42mg
- Carbohydrates: 59g
- Fiber: 12g
- Protein: 13g

# Raspberry Peach Smoothie Bowls

Gluten-free, quick & easy
Prep time: 5 minutes

**Ingredients:**

- 1½ cups plain nonfat Greek yogurt
- 1 cup frozen chopped mango
- 1/2 cup frozen banana slices
- 1/2 cup frozen raspberries
- 1/2 cup unsweetened almond milk
- 1 teaspoon vanilla extract
- 1 ripe peach, sliced (about 2/3 cup)
- 1/2 cup fresh raspberries
- 2 tablespoons sliced almonds
- 2 tablespoons chia seeds

**Method:**

1. Add the Greek yogurt, mango, banana, raspberries, almond milk, and vanilla to a blender and blend on low until the mixture reaches a soft serve consistency.
2. Scoop into two serving bowls and top each bowl with half the sliced peach, fresh raspberries, almonds, and chia seeds.
3. Enjoy immediately.

**Nutritional Content:**

- Calories: 422
- Fats: 9g
- Protein: 18g
- Cholesterol: 0mg
- Carbohydrates: 72g
- Fiber: 15g
- Sodium: 182mg

# Red Velvet Beet And Cherry Smoothie

Gluten-free, quick & easy
Prep time: 5 minutes

**Ingredients:**

- 1½ cups plain nonfat Greek yogurt
- 1 cup unsweetened almond milk
- 2 tablespoons unsweetened cocoa powder
- 1 cup frozen cherries
- 2/3 cup frozen banana slices
- 1/2 cup raw peeled and chopped beets
- 1/2 cup gluten-free rolled oats
- 2 pitted Medjool dates
- 1 teaspoon vanilla extract
- 1 cup ice cubes

**Method:**

1. Combine all the ingredients in a high-speed blender and blend until smooth.
2. Pour into two tall glasses and serve immediately.

**Nutritional Content:**

- Calories: 349
- Fats: 4g
- Protein: 17g
- Cholesterol: 4mg
- Carbohydrates: 65g
- Fiber: 9g
- Sodium: 248mg

# Chocolate Power Smoothie

Serves 2(1½ cups per serving)
Hands-on time: 10 min
Total time: 10 min

## Ingredients:

- 1 medium frozen banana
- 1 cup baby spinach
- 1 cup frozen blueberries
- 2 tablespoons unsweetened cocoa powder
- 2 tablespoons natural peanut butter
- 1½ cups vanilla soy milk
- 1 tablespoon hemp seeds
- 1/4 to 1/2 cup water (optional)

## Method:

1. If you don't have a very powerful blender, roughly chop the banana.
2. Combine the banana, spinach, blueberries, cocoa powder, peanut butter, soy milk, and hemp seeds in the blender, and purée very well. Add the water, a few tablespoons at a time, if you prefer a thinner consistency.

## Nutritional Content:

- Calories: 285
- Fats: 13g
- Cholesterol: 0mg
- Sodium: 180mg
- Carbohydrates: 37g
- Fiber: 8g
- Protein: 12g

# Banana Kefir Smoothie

Serves 2
Hands-on time: 5 min
Total time: 5 min

**Ingredients:**

- 1½ cups plain, unsweetened dairy kefir
- 2 small frozen bananas
- 2 teaspoons honey (optional)

**Method:**

1. Mix the kefir and bananas in a blender until smooth.
2. Taste, and add honey if needed.

**Nutritional Content:**

- Calories: 194
- Fats: 2g
- Cholesterol: 10mg
- Sodium: 82mg
- Carbohydrates: 38g
- Fiber: 3g
- Protein: 9g

# Strawberry Breakfast Sundae

Serves 2
Hands-on time: 5 min
Total time: 5 min

## Ingredients:

- 1 cup plain 2% Greek yogurt, divided
- 1 banana, sliced, divided
- 1/2 cup Omega-3 Skillet Granola or store-bought low-sugar granola, divided
- 1/4 cup slivered almonds, divided
- 1 cup strawberries, divided

## Method:

1. Divide the yogurt between two bowls.
2. Top each with half of the sliced banana, granola, almonds, and strawberries.

## Nutritional Content:

- Calories: 415
- Fats: 22g
- Cholesterol: 18mg
- Sodium: 91mg
- Carbohydrates: 33g
- Fiber: 7g
- Protein: 20g

# Banana Nut Muffins

Dairy-free
Prep time: 5 minutes
Cook time: 30 minutes

## Ingredients:

- Olive oil nonstick cooking spray
- 2/3 cup sliced very ripe banana
- 2 teaspoons granulated stevia or 2 tablespoons brown sugar
- 1/2 teaspoon baking soda
- 1/8 teaspoon salt
- 2 egg whites, beaten
- 1/4 cup unsweetened applesauce
- 1/2 teaspoon vanilla extract
- 1/2 cup whole-wheat pastry flour
- 4 tablespoons chopped walnuts

## Method:

1. Preheat the oven to 375°F and lightly spray two 7-ounce ramekins with the cooking spray.
2. In a large bowl, mash the banana with a fork, leaving some lumps for texture. Add the stevia, baking soda, and salt and whisk together for 1 minute.
3. Add the egg whites, applesauce, and vanilla and stir until combined. Add the flour and stir with a spatula until just combined.
4. Divide the batter evenly between the ramekins (they should be about half to three-quarters full), then sprinkle the walnuts evenly over the top. Bake for 25 to 30 minutes, or until the tops are golden brown and a toothpick inserted in the center comes out clean.
5. Let them cool for a few minutes, remove from the ramekins, and serve warm.

## Nutritional Content:

- Calories: 322
- Fats: 10g
- Protein: 11g
- Cholesterol: 0mg
- Carbohydrates: 49g
- Fiber: 4g
- Sodium: 500mg

# Peanut Butter And Raspberry Toast

Serves 1
Hands-on time: 5 min
Total time: 5 min

**Ingredients:**

- 1 slice sprouted-grain bread
- 2 tablespoons natural peanut butter
- 1 teaspoon hemp seeds (optional)
- 1/4 cup fresh raspberries

**Method:**

1. Toast the bread.
2. Spread the peanut butter on the toast. Sprinkle with hemp seeds (if using). Top with the raspberries.

**Nutritional Content:**

- Calories: 344
- Fats: 18g
- Cholesterol: 0mg
- Sodium: 184mg
- Carbohydrates: 29g
- Fiber: 8g
- Protein: 13g

# Omega-3 Skillet Granola

Serves 4(1/3 cup per serving)
Hands-on time: 10min
Total time: 10mi

## Ingredients:

- 2 tablespoons Better Butter or 1 tablespoon canola or sunflower oil plus
- 1 tablespoon unsalted butter
- 1 tablespoon honey
- 3/4 cup large-flake rolled oats
- 1/3 cup roughly chopped walnuts
- 1 tablespoon chia seeds
- 1 tablespoon hemp seeds
- 1 tablespoon ground flaxseed
- 1/2 teaspoon ground cinnamon
- Pinch salt

## Method:

1. In a large skillet, melt the Better Butter and honey over medium heat, then continue to cook until bubbly.
2. Stir in the oats, walnuts, chia seeds, hemp seeds, flaxseed, cinnamon, and salt and cook, stirring, until the oats and nuts start to brown, 3 to 4 minutes. If they're browning too fast, turn the heat down to medium-low.
3. Eat the granola right away or let it cool completely, then store in an airtight container for up to 2 weeks in the pantry or 3 months in the freezer.

## Nutritional Content:

- Calories: 230
- Fats: 16g
- Cholesterol: 8mg
- Sodium: 64mg
- Carbohydrates: 18g
- Fiber: 4g
- Protein: 5g

# Almost-Instant Oatmeal

Serves 2
Hands-on time: 5 min
Total time: 10 min

**Ingredients:**

- 2 cups vanilla soy milk, plus more if needed
- 3/4 cup oat bran
- 2 tablespoons natural peanut butter
- 2 teaspoons pure maple syrup
- 1/4 teaspoon ground cinnamon
- 1 banana, sliced, divided
- 1 tablespoon hemp seeds, divided

**Method:**

1. Heat the soy milk in a large pot over high heat. Add the oat bran, peanut butter, maple syrup, and cinnamon, stirring as you go. When it starts to boil, turn the heat down to medium-low.
2. Cook for 2 minutes, stirring occasionally. Add more milk or water if you prefer a thinner consistency.
3. Divided the oatmeal between two bowls. Top each with half of the sliced banana and hemp seeds.

**Nutritional Content:**

- Calories: 354
- Fats: 15g
- Cholesterol: 0mg
- Sodium: 123mg
- Carbohydrates: 54g
- Fiber: 9g
- Protein: 18g

# Apple-Pecan Oatmeal

Serves 2
Hands-on time: 10 min
Total time: 15 min

**Ingredients:**

- 1½ cups vanilla soy milk
- 2/3 cup old-fashioned oats
- 2 small apples
- 2 tablespoons ground flaxseed, divided
- 1/2 teaspoon ground cinnamon, divided
- 1/3 cup roughly chopped pecans, divided
- 2 tablespoons dried cherries, divided

**Method:**

1. Heat the soy milk and oats in a medium pot over high heat. When the milk starts to bubble, turn it down to medium-low and simmer.
2. Meanwhile, core and dice the apples. Add them to the pot as you go.
3. When the oats and apples are done to your liking, after about 10 minutes, divide the oatmeal between two bowls. Top each with half of the flaxseed and cinnamon, then half of the pecans and cherries.

**Nutritional Content:**

- Calories: 420
- Fats: 20g
- Cholesterol: 0mg
- Sodium: 92mg
- Carbohydrates: 56g
- Fiber: 11g
- Protein: 11g

# Blueberry-Banana Smoothie

Serves 2 (2 cups per serving)
Hands-on time: 10 min
Total time: 10 min

## Ingredients:

- 1 banana
- 1 cup frozen blueberries
- 1/2 cup frozen mango chunks
- 2 cups vanilla soy milk
- 1/2 cup plain 2% Greek yogurt
- 2 tablespoons hemp seeds

## Method:

1. Combine the banana, blueberries, mango, soy milk, yogurt, and hemp seeds in a blender, and blend well.

## Nutritional Content:

- Calories: 281
- Fats: 8g
- Cholesterol: 3mg
- Sodium: 141mg
- Carbohydrates: 41g
- Fiber: 5g
- Protein: 17g

# Pumpkin English Muffins

Dairy-free, gluten-free, quick & easy
Prep time: 1 minute
Cook time: 3 to 4 minutes

## Ingredients:

- Olive oil nonstick cooking spray
- 1/2 cup gluten-free oat flour
- 1 teaspoon baking powder
- 4 egg whites
- 1/4 cup pumpkin purée
- 1/2 teaspoon pumpkin pie spice
- 1/2 teaspoon ground cinnamon
- Pinch salt
- 1/2 to 1 teaspoon granulated stevia

## Method:

1. Spray two 7-ounce ramekins with the cooking spray.
2. In a medium bowl, stir together the oat flour, baking powder, egg whites, pumpkin purée, pumpkin pie spice, cinnamon, salt, and stevia until well combined.
3. Divide the batter evenly between the two ramekins.
4. Place one ramekin in the microwave and microwave on high for 1 minute to 1 minute 30 seconds (depending on your microwave), or until set. Repeat with the second ramekin.
5. Let the muffins cool for a moment, then remove them from the ramekins. Cut each English muffin in half horizontally and toast until done to your liking.
6. Enjoy with nut butter or the spread of your choice.

## Nutritional Content:

- Calories: 157
- Fats: 2g
- Protein: 11g
- Cholesterol: 0mg
- Carbohydrates: 25g
- Fiber: 4g
- Sodium: 149mg

# Chapter 3: Soups & Stews

## Broccoli And Gold Potato Soup

Dairy-free, gluten-free, vegan
Prep time: 10 minutes
Cook time: 35 minutes

**Ingredients:**

- 1 tablespoon olive oil
- 1/2 cup diced onion
- 1 garlic clove, minced
- 3 cups low-sodium vegetable broth
- 2 cups peeled and chopped Yukon gold potatoes
- 2 cups broccoli florets
- 1/4 teaspoon dried thyme
- 1/4 teaspoon red pepper flakes
- Salt
- Freshly ground black pepper
- 1/4 cup chopped fresh chives, for garnish

**Method:**

1. Heat the olive oil in a large saucepan over medium heat. Add the onion and garlic and cook 4 or 5 minutes until fragrant and translucent.
2. Add the vegetable broth and potatoes. Cover and bring to a boil. Decrease the heat to medium and cook for about 15 minutes, or until the potatoes are tender.
3. Add the broccoli, thyme, and red pepper flakes, cover, and steam for 5 minutes, or until the broccoli is cooked but still bright green.
4. Purée the soup in a blender or with an immersion blender. Season with salt and pepper.
5. Ladle into bowls, garnish with the chives, and serve.

**Nutritional Content:**

- Calories: 268
- Fats: 10g
- Protein: 13g
- Cholesterol: 0mg
- Carbohydrates: 35g
- Fiber: 7g
- Sodium: 587mg

# Simple Tomato Basil Soup

Dairy-free, gluten-free, vegan, quick & easy
Prep time: 5 minutes
Cook time: 10 minutes

## Ingredients:

- 1 teaspoon olive oil
- 1 cup chopped onion
- 4 garlic cloves, minced
- 7 cups chopped fresh tomatoes (aim for a mix of large, cherry, grape, and heirloom)
- 1/2 cup chopped fresh basil leaves
- 1/8 teaspoon salt
- 1 teaspoon freshly ground black pepper

## Method:

1. Heat the olive oil in a medium saucepan over medium heat. Add the onion and garlic and cook for 1 to 2 minutes.
2. Add the tomatoes and continue to cook, stirring every few minutes until the tomatoes have broken down and are soft.
3. Remove from the heat and add the basil, salt, and pepper.
4. Purée in a blender or use an immersion blender until smooth. Serve immediately.

## Nutritional Content:

- Calories: 169
- Fats: 4g
- Protein: 7g
- Cholesterol: 0mg
- Carbohydrates: 33g
- Fiber: 9g
- Sodium: 182mg

# Thai Seafood Soup

Dairy-free
Prep time: 20 minutes
Cook time: 20 minutes

## Ingredients:

- 1/2 tablespoon olive oil
- 2 garlic cloves, minced
- 1 cup sliced button mushrooms
- 1 cup julienned red bell pepper
- 2 cups low-sodium chicken broth
- 1/4 pound sea scallops, halved
- 1/4 cup thin diagonally sliced scallions
- 1/2 cup grated carrots
- 2 (2-inch) lengths lemongrass from bottom of stalk, smashed
- 6 ounces cod or haddock fillet, cut into 2 -inch chunks
- Zest of 1 lime
- 1/4 cup fresh cilantro leaves
- 1 teaspoon peeled and grated fresh ginger
- 1 teaspoon reduced-sodium soy sauce
- 1/2 teaspoon red pepper flakes

## Method:

1. Heat the olive oil in a large saucepan over medium heat. Add the garlic and sauté for 1 to 2 minutes. Add the mushrooms and sauté for 2 minutes. Add the bell pepper and sauté for 2 to 3 minutes, until softened.
2. Add the chicken broth, scallops, scallions, carrots, and lemongrass, and gently simmer for 5 minutes. Add the cod and lime zest and simmer for 5 minutes longer.
3. Stir in the cilantro, ginger, soy sauce, and red pepper flakes. Remove and discard the lemon-grass before serving.

## Nutritional Content:

- Calories: 256
- Fats: 6g
- Protein: 36g
- Cholesterol: 65mg
- Carbohydrates: 13g
- Fiber: 2g
- Sodium: 854mg

# Rustic Vegetable And Bean Soup

Dairy-free, gluten-free, vegan
Prep time: 10 minutes
Cook time: 35 minutes

## Ingredients:

- 1 tablespoon olive oil
- 1/2 cup chopped celery
- 1/2 cup chopped shallots
- Salt
- Freshly ground black pepper
- 2 garlic cloves, minced
- 1 tablespoon chopped fresh marjoram
- 1/2 cup chopped carrots
- 1/2 cup peeled and diced gold potatoes
- 1/2 cup chopped tomatoes, with juices reserved
- 3 cups low-sodium vegetable broth, divided
- 1 (15-ounce) can navy beans, drained and rinsed
- 2 teaspoons red wine vinegar
- 1/4 cup thinly sliced chives, for garnish

## Method:

1. Heat the olive oil in a 4-quart soup pot or Dutch oven over medium heat. Add the celery and shallots and season with a pinch of salt and freshly ground black pepper. Cook, stirring frequently, until the vegetables begin to soften but not brown, 4 to 6 minutes.
2. Add the garlic and marjoram and cook until fragrant, 1 minute more.
3. Add the carrots, potatoes, and tomatoes, stirring to incorporate with the seasonings and aromatics, then add 2 cups of broth, partially cover, and simmer until the vegetables are just barely tender, 10 to 20 minutes.
4. Add the beans, the reserved tomato juices, and the remaining 1 cup of broth. Stir to combine and simmer, partially covered, for 10 minutes to meld the flavors.
5. Taste the soup and adjust the seasoning with the vinegar, salt, and pepper.
6. Ladle the soup into bowls, garnish each serving with chives, and serve.

## Nutritional Content:

- Calories: 472
- Fats: 10g

- Protein: 28g
- Cholesterol: 0mg
- Carbohydrates: 69g

- Fiber: 16g
- Sodium: 323mg

# Two-Mushroom Barley Soup

Dairy-free, gluten-free, vegan
Prep time: 10 minutes
Cook time: 25 minutes

## Ingredients:

- 2 teaspoons olive oil
- 1 cup sliced carrots
- 1 cup diced onion
- 1/2 cup chopped celery
- 4 cups chopped button mushrooms
- 1 cup chopped shiitake mushrooms
- 2 garlic cloves, crushed
- 1½ teaspoons chopped fresh thyme
- 1/8 teaspoon salt
- 1/8 teaspoon freshly ground black pepper
- 2 cups nonfat milk or plant-based milk
- 1 cup water
- 1/3 cup quick-cooking barley

## Method:

1. Heat the olive oil in a large saucepan over medium heat. Add the carrots, onion, celery, button and shiitake mushrooms, garlic, thyme, salt, and pepper. Cook, stirring, for about 3 minutes, or until the vegetables release some of their juices. Increase the heat to medium-high and continue to cook, stirring often, for another 3 minutes, or until most of the liquid has evaporated.
2. Add the milk, water, and barley. Bring the mixture to a boil, stirring often. Decrease the heat and simmer, stirring occasionally, for about 15 minutes, or until the vegetables and barley are tender.
3. Ladle into bowls and enjoy immediately.

## Nutritional Content:

- Calories: 331
- Fats: 6g
- Protein: 18g
- Cholesterol: 5mg
- Carbohydrates: 54g
- Fiber: 10g
- Sodium: 384mg

# Garden Vegetable Stew With Toasted Cashews

Dairy-free, gluten-free, vegan
Prep time: 10 minutes
Cook time: 30 minutes

**Ingredients:**

- 1 tablespoon olive oil, plus 2 teaspoons, divided
- 1 small cayenne pepper, seeded and minced
- 1/2 cup chopped onion
- 1/2 cup chopped red bell pepper
- 2 garlic cloves, minced
- 2 teaspoons low-sodium tamari sauce
- 2 cups water
- 1/2 cup thinly sliced carrots
- 1/2 cup diced fresh tomato
- 1 cup chopped eggplant
- 1 cup sliced green beans
- 3/4 cup fresh corn kernels
- 1/2 cup raw cashews
- 1/2 cup thinly sliced shallots
- 2 cups chopped Swiss chard
- Salt
- Freshly ground black pepper

**Method:**

1. Heat 1 tablespoon of olive oil in a large saucepan over medium heat. Add the cayenne pepper, onion, bell pepper, and garlic and cook for about 2 minutes, or until very fragrant and the onion has softened slightly.
2. Add the tamari and water. Bring to a boil, then add the carrots. Decrease the heat and simmer for 3 minutes.
3. Add the tomato and eggplant and cook for 1 minute. Add the green beans and corn and cook for 2 to 3 more minutes. Decrease the heat to low.
4. Meanwhile, in a small sauté pan, heat 1 teaspoon of olive oil over medium-low heat. Add the cashews to the pan and toast them for 4 to 5 minutes, or until they brown on all sides. Transfer them to a small plate.
5. Return the sauté pan to the heat and add the remaining 1 teaspoon of olive oil. Add the shallots to the pan and stir for 10 to 15 minutes, or until they turn a deep brown and crisp in some areas. Set them aside.
6. Bring the pot of stew back to a boil and add the Swiss chard. Cook until the greens wilt, about 1 minute. Season with salt and pepper.
7. Ladle the stew into serving bowls, top each bowl with toasted cashews and some shallots, and serve.

## Nutritional Content:

- Calories: 457
- Fats: 29g
- Protein: 12g
- Cholesterol: 0mg

- Carbohydrates: 47g
- Fiber: 9g
- Sodium: 500mg

# Moroccan Spiced Red Lentil And Millet Stew

Dairy-free, gluten-free, vegan
Prep time: 10 minutes
Cook time: 50 minutes

**Ingredients:**

- 1/2 tablespoon olive oil
- 1/2 cup finely chopped onion
- 3 cups low-sodium vegetable broth
- 1/3 cup dry millet
- 1 cup dried lentils, rinsed
- 1 celery stalk, chopped
- 1/2 cup finely chopped red bell pepper
- 2 tablespoons tomato paste
- 1/8 teaspoon cayenne pepper
- 1 teaspoon ground coriander
- 1/2 teaspoon ground cumin
- 1/4 teaspoon ground cinnamon
- 1/2 cup chopped dried apricots
- Salt

**Method:**

1. Heat the olive oil in a 3-quart stockpot or saucepan over medium heat. Add the onion and cook stirring frequently, until the onion is fragrant, about 6 minutes.
2. Add the broth, millet, and lentils. Bring the mixture to a boil.
3. Add the celery, bell pepper, tomato paste, cayenne, coriander, cumin, cinnamon, dried apricots, and salt to taste. Turn down the heat, cover and let simmer for 35 to 45 minutes, or until the lentils and millet are tender.
4. Serve hot.

**Nutritional Content:**

- Calories: 573
- Fats: 7g
- Protein: 33g
- Cholesterol: 0mg
- Carbohydrates: 96g
- Fiber: 35g
- Sodium: 429mg

# Slow Cooker Chicken Vegetable Stew

Dairy-free
Prep time: 10 minutes
Cook time: 4 hours

## Ingredients:

- 1 skinless, boneless chicken breast, trimmed and cut into 1/2-inch cubes
- 1 cup cauliflower florets
- 3/4 cup sliced carrots
- 1/2 cup halved button mushrooms
- 1/2 cup chopped onion
- 1/4 cup diced celery
- 2 garlic cloves, minced
- 2 cups low-sodium chicken broth
- 1 bay leaf
- 1/4 teaspoon freshly ground black pepper

## Method:

1. Add the chicken, cauliflower, carrots, mushrooms, onion, celery, and garlic to the insert of a 3.5-quart slow cooker. Add the chicken broth, bay leaf, and pepper. Add some water if the mixture looks too thick.
2. Cook on the low heat setting for 4 hours.
3. Ladle into bowls and serve.

## Nutritional Content:

- Calories: 257
- Fats: 8g
- Protein: 32g
- Cholesterol: 75mg
- Carbohydrates: 12g
- Fiber: 3g
- Sodium: 356mg

# Sweet Potato And Black Bean Chili

Dairy-free, gluten-free, vegan, quick & easy
Prep time: 5 minutes
Cook time: 20 minutes

## Ingredients:

- 2 teaspoons olive oil
- 1 cup peeled and diced sweet potato
- 1/2 cup finely sliced onion
- 1/2 cup diced red bell pepper
- 2 garlic cloves, minced
- 1 tablespoon chili powder
- 2 teaspoons ground cumin
- 1 teaspoon smoked paprika
- 1/8 teaspoon salt
- 1⅓ cups water
- 1 (15-ounce) can black beans, drained and rinsed
- 1 cup diced tomatoes, with juice
- 2 teaspoons freshly squeezed lime juice
- 2 tablespoons chopped fresh cilantro

## Method:

1. Heat the olive oil in a large saucepan over medium-high heat. Add the sweet potato, onion, and bell pepper and cook for about 4 minutes, stirring often, or until the onion has slightly softened.
2. Add the garlic, chili powder, cumin, paprika, and salt and cook for about 30 seconds, stirring constantly, or until fragrant. Add the water and simmer, covered, for 10 to 12 minutes, until the sweet potato is tender.
3. Add the beans, tomatoes and their juices, and lime juice and return to a simmer, stirring often. Decrease the heat and simmer for about 4 minutes, or until slightly reduced.
4. Remove from the heat, stir in the cilantro, and serve.

## Nutritional Content:

- Calories: 475
- Fats: 7g
- Protein: 24g
- Cholesterol: 0mg
- Carbohydrates: 84g
- Fiber: 25g
- Sodium: 234mg

# Hearty White Bean And Kale Soup

Dairy-free, gluten-free, vegan, quick & easy
Prep time: 10 minutes
Cook time: 20 minutes

**Ingredients:**

- 1 tablespoon olive oil
- 1 cup finely sliced onion
- 1/2 cup diced red bell pepper
- 1/4 cup diced celery
- 4 garlic cloves, thinly sliced
- 1 tablespoon chopped fresh rosemary leaves
- 3 cups low-sodium vegetable broth
- 1 bay leaf
- 1 (15-ounce) can white beans, drained and rinsed
- 2 cups packed, stemmed, and finely chopped kale Salt
- Freshly ground black pepper
- 2 teaspoons freshly squeezed lemon juice

**Method:**

1. Heat the olive oil in a medium saucepan over medium-high heat. Add the onion, bell pepper, celery, garlic, and rosemary. Cook, stirring often, for about 4 minutes, or until the onions and garlic have softened but not browned.
2. Add the broth, bay leaf, and beans. Bring to a boil, reduce to a slow simmer, and cook for 10 minutes.
3. Add the kale and continue to cook for about 5 minutes until it is completely wilted.
4. Season with salt and pepper. Stir in the lemon juice and serve immediately.

**Nutritional Content:**

- Calories: 531
- Fats: 10g
- Protein: 34g
- Cholesterol: 0mg
- Carbohydrates: 79g
- Fiber: 18g
- Sodium: 865mg

# Chapter 4: Vegetarian

## Sprouted-Grain Pizza Toast

Serves 2
Hands-on time: 22min
Total time: 30min

**Ingredients:**

- 1 tablespoon canola or sunflower oil
- 4 slices sprouted-grain bread
- 2 tablespoons extra-virgin olive oil
- 1/2 teaspoon stir-in garlic paste
- 1/2 cup shredded mozzarella cheese
- 1/2 cup cherry tomatoes, thinly sliced, divided
- 1/4 cup fresh basil leaves, stacked, rolled, and thinly sliced, divided

**Method:**

1. Preheat the oven to 400°F.
2. Brush a thin layer of canola or sunflower oil on a baking sheet. Spread out the bread on the sheet. Toast in the oven for 2½ minutes, flip the bread over and toast for 2½ minutes more.
3. Meanwhile, mix the olive oil and garlic paste in a small bowl.
4. Remove the toast from the oven, and brush some garlic oil on each slice. Add some mozzarella to each slice. Top each with half of the cherry tomatoes and basil.
5. Toast for another 5 minutes, until the cheese is melted and the crust is just starting to brown.

**Nutritional Content:**

- Calories: 480
- Fats: 28g
- Cholesterol: 18mg
- Sodium: 548mg
- Carbohydrates: 41g
- Fiber: 8g
- Protein: 17g

# Black Bean Quesadillas

Serves 4
Hands-on time: 25min
Total-on time: 25min

**Ingredients:**

- 1 (15-ounce) can no-salt-added black beans, rinsed and drained
- 1/4 cup Fresh Tomato Salsa or lower-sodium store-bought salsa
- 3/4 cup shredded Cheddar cheese, divided
- 1 red bell pepper, seeded and chopped, divided
- 2 tablespoons canola or sunflower oil, divided
- 4 large, whole-grain tortillas

**Method:**

1. Blend the beans and salsa together in a food processor. If you don't have a food processor, mash them in a large bowl with a fork or a potato masher.
2. Spread one-fourth of the bean mixture (about 1/2 cup) on each tortilla. Sprinkle each with 3 tablespoons of cheese and one-fourth of the bell pepper (about 1/4 cup). Fold in half.
3. Preheat a large, heavy skillet over medium heat. Add 1 tablespoon of oil to the skillet and spread it around. Place the first two quesadillas in the skillet. Cover and cook until the quesadillas are crispy on the bottom, about 2 minutes. Flip and cook until crispy on the other side, about 2 minutes more.
4. Use the remaining 1 tablespoon of oil to cook the remaining two quesadillas, keeping the first two warm in the oven if needed.

**Nutritional Content:**

- Calories: 415
- Fats: 22g
- Cholesterol: 18mg
- Sodium: 91mg
- Carbohydrates: 33g
- Fiber: 7g
- Protein: 20g

# Tofu Kale Scramble

Dairy-free, gluten-free, vegan, quick & easy
Prep time: 15 minutes
Cook time: 15 minutes

## Ingredients:

- 1/2 teaspoon olive oil
- 1/3 cup diced red bell pepper
- 1/2 cup packed, stemmed, and chopped kale
- 1/4 cup diced scallions, plus more for garnish
- 1 (14-ounce) block extra-firm tofu, pressed for 10 to 15 minutes
- 1/2 cup diced fresh tomato
- 1 tablespoon plus 1 teaspoon nutritional yeast
- 1/4 teaspoon onion powder
- 1/4 teaspoon garlic powder
- 1/8 teaspoon salt
- 1/8 teaspoon freshly ground black pepper
- 1/4 cup diced avocado
- 1/4 teaspoon turmeric, for color (optional)

## Method:

1. Heat the olive oil in a large sauté pan over medium heat.
2. Add the bell pepper, kale, and scallions to the pan and sauté for about 3 minutes, or until the kale turns bright green and is slightly wilted.
3. Crumble the block of tofu into approximately 1/2-inch chunks and fold them into the vegetables.
4. Stir in the tomato, nutritional yeast, onion powder, garlic powder, salt, and pepper and simmer over medium-low heat for 2 to 3 minutes.
5. Add the diced avocado and turmeric (if using) and stir for 1 to 2 minutes, just long enough to heat the avocado through.
6. Serve the scramble garnished with some diced scallions.

## Nutritional Content:

- Calories: 206
- Fats: 9g
- Protein: 21g
- Cholesterol: 0mg
- Carbohydrates: 14g
- Fiber: 5g
- Sodium: 287mg

# Indian Spiced Cauliflower Fried "Rice"

Dairy-free, gluten-free, quick & easy
Prep time: 10 minutes
Cook time: 10 minutes

## Ingredients:

- 2 teaspoons olive oil, divided
- 2 eggs, beaten
- 2 garlic cloves, finely minced
- 1/4 cup finely chopped red bell pepper
- 1/4 cup finely chopped carrots
- 1/4 cup finely chopped onion
- 3 cups grated cauliflower
- 1 cup frozen shelled edamame
- 1/2 teaspoon ground cumin
- 1/4 teaspoon ground ginger
- 1/8 teaspoon ground cardamom
- 1/8 teaspoon ground cinnamon
- 1/8 teaspoon salt
- Freshly ground black pepper
- 1 cup finely chopped fresh spinach
- 1 tablespoon Bragg's liquid aminos (or low-sodium soy sauce)
- 1/4 cup cashews, for garnish

## Method:

1. Heat 1 teaspoon of olive oil in a large sauté pan. Add the eggs and slowly stir until curds form, then fold the curds over themselves until there is no more liquid egg. Remove from the heat and break into small pieces. Transfer the eggs to a plate.
2. Heat the remaining 1 teaspoon of olive oil. Add the garlic and sauté for 30 seconds. Add the bell pepper, carrots, and onion and sauté for 2 minutes. Add the cauliflower, edamame, cumin, ginger, cardamom, cinnamon, salt, and a few grinds of pepper and cook, stirring, for 5 to 8 minutes. Add the spinach and cook until wilted, about 2 minutes.
3. Add the Bragg's aminos and the cooked egg and stir well to combine. Remove from the heat and divide equally between two bowls. Sprinkle with the cashews and serve.

## Nutritional Content:

- Calories: 458
- Fats: 26g
- Protein: 29g
- Cholesterol: 164mg
- Carbohydrates: 34g
- Fiber: 11g

- Sodium: 1,622mg

# Pile-It-High Veggie Sandwich

Serves 2
Hands-on time: 15 min
Total time: 15 min

## Ingredients:

- 2 teaspoons red wine vinegar
- 1 teaspoon extra-virgin olive oil
- 1/4 teaspoon ground cumin
- 1/3 cup shredded carrot (about 1 carrot)
- 2 tablespoons hummus, divided
- 4 slices whole-grain multigrain bread
- 1/2 avocado, sliced
- 6 (1/2-inch-thick) slices Simple Roasted Peppers or jarred roasted red peppers, drained well
- 4 green lettuce leaves

## Method:

1. In a small bowl, whisk together the vinegar, oil, and cumin. Add the carrot and toss well, then set aside to marinate for 10 minutes.
2. Spread 1 tablespoon of hummus on each of two slices of bread.
3. Divide the avocado slices between the other two pieces of bread. Top with the roasted peppers and lettuce.
4. Drain the carrots, and add them on top of the lettuce. Close the sandwiches and enjoy.

## Nutritional Content:

- Calories: 384
- Fats: 16g
- Cholesterol: 0mg
- Sodium: 463mg
- Carbohydrates: 48g
- Fiber: 11g
- Protein: 14g

# Crunchy Peanut Fried Rice

Serves 4
Hands-on time: 20min
Total time: 25min

**Ingredients:**

- 2 tablespoons reduced-sodium soy sauce
- 3 tablespoons rice vinegar
- 1 tablespoon sugar
- 5 large eggs
- 2 tablespoons peanut oil
- 3 cups cooked brown rice
- 1/2 cup frozen peas
- 1 (14-ounce) bag coleslaw mix
- 1 teaspoon minced fresh ginger
- 3 garlic cloves, chopped
- 1/2 cup roughly chopped lightly salted peanuts

**Method:**

1. Mix the soy sauce, vinegar, and sugar in a small bowl. Set aside.
2. Crack the eggs into a bowl, and beat gently.
3. Heat the oil in a large skillet over high heat. When it is hot, add the rice and stir-fry for 2 minutes. Add the peas and coleslaw mix, and cook for 3 minutes. Add the ginger, and garlic and cook for 1 more minute.
4. Turn the heat down to medium. Push the vegetables and rice to the side, and add the eggs. Stir until lightly scrambled.
5. Pour the sauce over the rice and eggs, and mix well. Top with the peanuts.

**Nutritional Content:**

- Calories: 508
- Fats: 24g
- Cholesterol: 233mg
- Sodium: 494mg
- Carbohydrates: 56g
- Fiber: 7g
- Protein: 20g

# Chickpea-Almond Curry

Serves 4
Hands-on time: 30 min
Total time: 30 min

**Ingredients:**

- 1 tablespoon canola or sunflower oil
- 1 onion, chopped
- 2 cups stir-fry vegetables, fresh or frozen
- 1 tablespoon grated fresh ginger
- 2 teaspoons red or green curry paste
- 1 teaspoon ground turmeric
- 1 (14-ounce) can diced no-salt-added tomatoes
- 1 (15-ounce) can no-salt-added-chickpeas, rinsed and drained
- 1/4 cup smooth almond butter
- 2 cups reduced-sodium vegetable broth

**Method:**

1. Heat the oil in a large skillet over medium-high heat. When it is hot, add the onion and cook until translucent, 4 to 5 minutes. Add the stir-fry vegetables, and cook for 3 to 4 minutes. Add the ginger, curry paste, and turmeric, and cook for 1 more minute.
2. Stir in the tomatoes with their juice, chickpeas, almond butter, and broth, and bring to a boil. Turn the heat down to low and simmer, stirring occasionally, for 5 to 10 minutes, until warmed through.

**Nutritional Content:**

- Calories: 308
- Fats: 14g
- Cholesterol: 0mg
- Sodium: 348mg
- Carbohydrates: 34g
- Fiber: 10g
- Protein: 12g

# Loaded Sweet Potatoes

Dairy-free, gluten-free, vegan
Prep time: 5 minutes
Cook time: 80 minutes

**Ingredients:**

- 2 medium sweet potatoes
- 1/2 tablespoon olive oil
- 1 garlic clove, minced
- 4 cups stemmed and chopped kale leaves
- 1/2 cup halved grape tomatoes
- 1/3 cup water
- 1 (15-ounce) can black beans, drained and rinsed
- Salt
- Freshly ground black pepper
- 1/2 avocado. peeled. seeded. and sliced

**Method:**

1. Preheat the oven to 375°F and line a baking sheet with parchment paper.
2. Using a fork, poke multiple holes into both sweet potatoes. Place the sweet potatoes on the baking sheet and bake for 45 to 60 minutes, or until tender.
3. In the meantime, heat the olive oil in a medium saucepan over medium heat. Add the garlic and cook for 1 minute, or until fragrant, taking care not to brown it. Add the kale and tomatoes and toss to coat. Add the water, cover, and cook for 5 minutes. Stir the vegetables, decrease the heat, and cook, uncovered, 15 minutes more until the kale is bright green and slightly wilted.
4. Add the beans and cook until warmed through. Season with salt and pepper.
5. Cut the sweet potatoes in half lengthwise. Top with the black bean-kale mixture and sliced avocado. Serve hot.

**Nutritional Content:**

- Calories: 751
- Fats: 15g
- Protein: 28g
- Cholesterol: 0mg
- Carbohydrates: 133g
- Fiber:33g
- Sodium: 163mg

# Polenta With Tomatoes And Black Beans

Serves 3
Hands-on time: 25min
Total time: 25min

## Ingredients:

- 1 tablespoon extra-virgin olive oil
- 1 small yellow onion, chopped
- 2 garlic cloves, minced
- 1 teaspoon dried thyme
- 1 (15-ounce) can no-salt-added black beans, rinsed and drained
- 1 (14-ounce) can no-salt-added diced tomatoes
- 2/3 cup cornmeal (also called corn grits)
- 2 ⅔ cups water, divided
- 1 bunch spinach, large stems removed
- 1/2 cup grated Parmesan cheese

## Method:

1. Heat the oil in a large sauté pan over medium heat. Sauté the onion, garlic, and thyme until the onion is soft, 3 to 5 minutes. Add the beans and the tomatoes with their juice, and simmer over a low heat while you cook the polenta.
2. Combine the cornmeal with 2/3 cup of water in a small bowl. Set aside.
3. In a small saucepan, bring the remaining 2 cups of water to a boil over high heat. Reduce the heat to low, and stir in the cornmeal-water mixture. Stir frequently until the polenta is smooth and creamy, about 10 minutes, adding more water if needed.
4. When the polenta is ready, stir the spinach into the beans and tomatoes, cover, and cook until the spinach is wilted, about 2 minutes. Stir to incorporate.
5. Spoon the polenta into bowls, and top with the beans, tomatoes, and spinach. Sprinkle with the Parmesan.

## Nutritional Content:

- Calories: 387
- Fats: 10g
- Cholesterol: 9mg
- Sodium: 263mg
- Carbohydrates: 57g
- Fiber: 11g
- Protein: 18g

# Pantry Beans And Rice

Serves 3
Hands-on time: 25min
Total time: 25min

## Ingredients:

- 3/4 cup uncooked parboiled brown rice
- 2 teaspoons extra-virgin olive oil
- 1 cup fresh or frozen chopped onion
- 1 (15-ounce) can no-salt-added pinto beans, rinsed and drained
- 1 (14-ounce) can no-salt-added diced tomatoes
- 2/3 cup spicy salsa
- 1 cup frozen broccoli florets
- 1 tablespoon freshly squeezed lime juice
- 2/3 cup shredded aged Cheddar cheese
- 1/2 teaspoon red pepper flakes (optional)

## Method:

1. Cook the rice according to the package directions.
2. In a large skillet, heat the oil over medium-high heat. Add the onion and cook until soft, 4 to 5 minutes. Then add the beans, tomatoes with their juice, and salsa. Bring to a boil.
3. Add the broccoli, and when the liquid returns to a boil, turn the heat to low and simmer for 2 to 3 minutes. Remove from the heat when the broccoli is crisp-tender but still bright green.
4. Add the rice when it's done cooking. Stir in the lime juice, and top with the shredded Cheddar and red pepper flakes (if using).

## Nutritional Content:

- Calories: 479
- Fats: 14g
- Cholesterol: 25mg
- Sodium: 442mg
- Carbohydrates: 72g
- Fiber: 13g
- Protein: 20g

# Spicy Spinach And Almond Stir-Fry

Dairy-free, quick & easy
Prep time: 10 minutes
Cook time: 10 minutes

## Ingredients:

- 3 teaspoons olive oil, divided 2 eggs, beaten
- 2 garlic cloves, minced
- 3/4 cup chopped scallions
- 1 cup thinly sliced Brussels sprouts
- 4 cups baby spinach
- 1/4 cup sliced almonds
- 2 cups cooked and chilled brown rice
- 2 teaspoons reduced-sodium tamari or soy sauce
- 2 teaspoons sriracha
- 1 lime, halved
- 1/4 cup chopped fresh cilantro, for garnish

## Method:

1. Heat a large (12-inch or wider) wok or nonstick frying pan over medium-high heat. Once the pan is hot enough that a drop of water sizzles on contact, add 1 teaspoon of olive oil. Pour in the eggs and cook, stirring occasionally, until the eggs are scrambled and lightly set, about 3 minutes. Transfer the eggs to a medium bowl.
2. Add 1 teaspoon of olive oil to the pan and add the garlic, scallions, and Brussels sprouts. Cook, stirring frequently, for 30 seconds, or until fragrant. Add the spinach and continue to cook, stirring frequently, for about 2 minutes, or until the spinach is wilted and tender. Transfer the mixture to the bowl of eggs.
3. Add the almonds to the pan and cook, stirring frequently, for about 1 minute, or until they are crisp and lightly browned. Add the remaining 1 teaspoon of olive oil and the rice to the pan and cook, stirring occasionally, for about 3 minutes until the rice is hot.
4. Pour the contents of the bowl back into the pan. Add the tamari, sriracha, and juice from half a lime. Stir to combine and remove from the heat.
5. Cut the remaining lime half into wedges then divide the stir-fry into individual bowls. Garnish with the lime wedges and a sprinkling of cilantro. Serve immediately.

## Nutritional Content:

- Calories: 587
- Fats: 20g

- Protein: 20g
- Cholesterol: 164mg
- Carbohydrates: 86g
- Fiber: 9g
- Sodium: 557mg

# Portobello Mushrooms With Mozzarella And Onions

Gluten-free
Prep time: 10 minutes
Cook time: 50 minutes

## Ingredients:

- 1/2 tablespoon olive oil
- 1½ cups diced onion
- Salt
- Freshly ground black pepper
- 2 portobello mushrooms, stems removed
- 6 tablespoons shredded part-skim mozzarella cheese
- 1 cup sliced zucchini

## Method:

1. Preheat the oven to 350°F and line a baking pan with parchment paper.
2. Heat the olive oil in a medium saucepan over medium heat. Add the onion and cook for about 20 minutes, or until soft and browned. If the onions begin to stick, add a little water and cook until the water evaporates. Season with salt and pepper.
3. Place the mushrooms in the baking pan, stemmed-side up. Pack half of the cooked onions and half of the mozzarella in each mushroom cap.
4. Arrange the sliced zucchini beside the mushrooms in the baking pan. Season with salt and pepper. Bake for 30 minutes and serve warm.

## Nutritional Content:

- Calories: 356
- Fats: 20g
- Protein: 31g
- Cholesterol: 45mg
- Carbohydrates: 19g
- Fiber: 6g
- Sodium: 609mg

# Pocket Eggs With Sesame Sauce

Dairy-free, quick & easy
Prep time: 5 minutes
Cook time: 5 minutes

**Ingredients:**

- 2 teaspoons low-sodium soy sauce
- 1 teaspoon sesame oil
- 1½ tablespoons rice vinegar
- 1 tablespoon minced scallions
- 2 teaspoons olive oil
- 4 large eggs
- 1 tablespoon black or white sesame seeds
- 1 tablespoon dried basil
- 1/4 teaspoon freshly ground black pepper

**Method:**

1. In a small bowl, whisk together the soy sauce, sesame oil, vinegar, and scallions. Set it aside.
2. Heat the olive oil in a medium nonstick skillet over medium heat and swirl to coat. Crack 2 eggs into a small bowl then crack the remaining 2 eggs into a second small bowl.
3. Working quickly, pour 2 eggs on one side of the skillet and the other 2 on the opposite side of the skillet. The egg whites will flow together, forming one large piece.
4. Sprinkle the sesame seeds, basil, and pepper over the eggs. Cook until the egg whites are crispy and golden brown on the bottom and the yolks are firmly set, about 3 minutes. Keeping them in one piece, flip the eggs using a wide spatula and cook until the whites turn crispy and golden brown on the other side, 1 to 2 minutes more.
5. Pour the reserved sauce over the eggs. Simmer for 30 seconds, turning the eggs once to coat both sides with sauce. Serve in wedges, drizzled with the pan sauce.

**Nutritional Content:**

- Calories: 241
- Fats: 19g
- Protein: 14g
- Cholesterol: 372mg
- Carbohydrates: 3g
- Fiber: 1g
- Sodium: 440mg

# Chickpeas, Tomatoes, And Swiss Chard

Serves 4
Hands-on time: 20min
Total time: 20min

## Ingredients:

- 1 bunch Swiss chard
- 2 tablespoons extra-virgin olive oil
- 1 onion, thinly sliced
- 2 garlic cloves, minced
- 1 teaspoon ground cumin
- 1/2 teaspoon red pepper flakes
- 1 (14-ounce) can diced tomatoes seasoned with basil and garlic
- 1 (15-ounce) can no-salt-added chickpeas, rinsed and drained
- Zest and juice of 1 lemon (about 3 tablespoons juice)
- 1/2 cup chopped walnuts
- Freshly ground black pepper

## Method:

1. Trim the chard, then chop the stems and leaves; keep the stems and leaves separate.
2. Heat the oil in a large skillet over medium heat. When it is hot, add the onion and garlic and cook, stirring occasionally, for 3 to 4 minutes.
3. Add the chard stems and continue to cook until the onion is softened, 3 to 4 minutes more.
4. Add the cumin and red pepper flakes, and cook for 1 minute. Add the tomatoes with their juice and the chickpeas, and cook until warm, 3 to 4 minutes.
5. Add the chard leaves, cover, and cook until wilted, about 2 minutes.
6. Remove from the heat, and add the lemon zest and juice, walnuts, and pepper.

## Nutritional Content:

- Calories: 317
- Fats: 18g
- Cholesterol: 0mg
- Sodium: 482mg
- Carbohydrates: 31g
- Fiber: 9g
- Protein: 11g

# Savory Cheesy Rosemary Oatmeal

Gluten-free, quick & easy
Prep time: 5 minutes
Cook time: 15 minutes

**Ingredients:**

- 1 cup gluten-free rolled oats
- 1 cup water
- 1 cup unsweetened almond milk or nonfat milk
- 2/3 cup frozen green peas
- 1 teaspoon olive oil
- 1/2 cup sliced button mushrooms
- 1 cup firmly packed chopped baby spinach
- 1 cup chopped tomato
- 1 tablespoon fresh rosemary
- 1/2 cup part-skim ricotta cheese
- Salt
- Freshly ground black pepper

**Method:**

1. In a medium pot over medium heat, bring the oats, water, and almond milk to a boil, stirring occasionally. Add the peas, decrease the heat to medium low, and cook for 1 to 2 minutes, stirring often to prevent sticking and burning. Decrease the heat to low.
2. Meanwhile, heat the olive oil in a medium skillet over medium heat. Add the mushrooms and spinach and sauté for 3 to 4 minutes, or until the mushrooms start to release their liquid and the spinach is slightly wilted.
3. Add the tomato and rosemary to the mushroom-spinach mixture and cook for 3 minutes.
4. Add the ricotta to the oats and stir to combine. Transfer the vegetable mixture to the oat mixture and stir until well incorporated. Season with salt and pepper and serve warm.

**Nutritional Content:**

- Calories: 393
- Fats: 11g
- Protein: 21g
- Cholesterol: 22mg
- Carbohydrates: 50g
- Fiber: 9g
- Sodium: 243mg

# Chapter 5: Poultry

## Baked Mustard-Lime Chicken

Dairy-free, gluten-free
Prep time:10 minutes, plus at least 15 minutes
Chilling time cook time: 20 minutes

### Ingredients:

- 1/4 cup freshly squeezed lime juice
- 1/4 cup chopped fresh cilantro
- 2 garlic cloves, minced
- 2 tablespoons Dijon mustard
- 1/2 tablespoon olive oil
- 1/2 tablespoon chili powder
- 1/8 teaspoon salt
- 1/4 teaspoon freshly ground black pepper
- 2 (4-ounce) skinless, boneless chicken breasts

### Method:

1. Preheat the oven to 350°F.
2. Add the lime juice, cilantro, garlic, mustard, olive oil, chili powder, salt, and pepper to a food processor and pulse until the ingredients are well combined.
3. Place the chicken breasts in a 7-by-11-inch glass oven-proof baking dish. Pour the marinade over the chicken, cover, and refrigerate for at least 15 minutes or up to 6 hours.
4. Bake, uncovered, for 18 to 20 minutes, or until an instant-read thermometer registers 165°F. Serve immediately.

### Nutritional Content:

- Calories: 189
- Fats: 5g
- Protein: 27g
- Cholesterol: 65mg
- Carbohydrates: 4g
- Fiber: 2g
- Sodium: 423mg

# Artichoke And Zucchini Chicken Thighs

Serves 4
Hands-on time: 20 min
Total time: 20min

**Ingredients:**

- 1 cup uncooked quinoa
- 2 teaspoons unsalted butter
- 1 pound boneless, skinless chicken thighs, cut into bite-size
- pieces
- 2 medium zucchini, cut into bite-size pieces
- 1 garlic clove, minced (optional)
- 1 (12-ounce) jar quartered marinated artichoke hearts, drained
- 1 tablespoon freshly squeezed lemon juice
- 1/4 cup grated Parmesan cheese (optional)
- 1/4 cup minced fresh flat-leaf parsley (optional)

**Method:**

1. Cook the quinoa according to the package directions.
2. Meanwhile, heat the butter in a large skillet over medium-high heat. When the butter is hot, add the chicken and cook until brown, about 2 minutes on each side. Add the zucchini and garlic (if using), and cook until the chicken and zucchini are cooked through, 5 to 10 minutes. The chicken should be opaque with mostly clear juices. Add the artichoke hearts and cook just long enough to warm them up.
3. Remove from the heat and sprinkle with the lemon juice, cheese, and parsley (if using). Serve over the quinoa.

**Nutritional Content:**

- Calories: 388
- Fats: 11g
- Cholesterol: 115mg
- Sodium: 429mg
- Carbohydrates: 39g
- Fiber: 8g
- Protein: 34g

# Balsamic Rosemary Chicken

Dairy-free, gluten-free
Prep time: 10 minutes, plus 45 minutes chilling time
Cook time: 35 minutes

## Ingredients:

- 1/2 cup balsamic vinegar, plus 2 tablespoons
- 1 teaspoon olive oil
- 1 tablespoon chopped fresh rosemary
- 1 garlic clove, minced
- 1/8 teaspoon salt
- Freshly ground black pepper
- Olive oil cooking spray
- 2 (6-ounce) boneless, skinless chicken breasts
- Fresh rosemary sprigs, for garnish

## Method:

1. In a small saucepan, stir together 1/2 cup of balsamic vinegar, the olive oil, rosemary, garlic, salt, and pepper. Bring to a boil, lower the heat to medium, and simmer for about 3 minutes, or until reduced by half. Transfer the pan to the refrigerator for about 15 minutes or the freezer for about 5 minutes.
2. Coat a 9-by-9-inch baking dish with cooking spray. Place the chicken in the baking dish and pour the cooled marinade over the chicken. Refrigerate for 30 minutes.
3. Preheat the oven to 400°F. Remove the dish from the refrigerator, cover it with aluminum foil and bake the chicken in the marinade for 35 minutes, or until an instant-read thermometer registers 165°F.
4. Transfer the chicken to serving plates. Pour the cooked marinade into a small saucepan. Add the remaining 2 tablespoons of balsamic vinegar and cook for 3 to 5 minutes, or until the sauce has thickened. Pour the sauce over the chicken and serve garnished with fresh rosemary.

## Nutritional Content:

- Calories: 228
- Fats: 4g
- Protein: 39g
- Cholesterol: 97mg
- Carbohydrates: 2g
- Fiber: 1g
- Sodium: 261mg

# Weeknight Coq Au Vin

Serves 4
Hands-on time: 25 min
Total time: 30 min

**Ingredients:**

- 2 tablespoons Better Butter or 1 tablespoon unsalted butter plus
- 1 tablespoon extra-virgin olive oil
- 1 pound boneless, skinless chicken thighs, pounded to 1/2-inch thickness
- 1/4 teaspoon kosher salt
- Freshly ground black pepper
- 3 large carrots, peeled and thinly sliced on the diagonal
- 8 ounces sliced mushrooms
- 1 yellow onion, sliced
- 1 cup dry red wine
- 1 cup reduced-sodium chicken broth
- 1 tablespoon tomato paste
- 3 fresh thyme sprigs

**Method:**

1. Melt the Better Butter in a heavy skillet over medium-high heat. Sprinkle the chicken with salt and pepper. When the butter starts to froth, add the chicken, and brown for 1 to 2 minutes on each side. Transfer to a plate.
2. Add the carrots, mushrooms, and onion to the skillet. Sauté until the onion starts to soften, 3 to 4 minutes, then add the wine, broth, tomato paste, and thyme. Cook until the vegetables are just crisp-tender, 7 to 8 minutes.
3. Return the chicken to the pan, and simmer until cooked through, 5 to 10 minutes. It should be opaque with mostly clear juices. Remove the thyme and serve.

**Nutritional Content:**

- Calories: 296
- Fats: 12g
- Cholesterol: 115mg
- Sodium: 295mg
- Carbohydrates: 11g
- Fiber: 2g
- Protein: 26g

# Almost Chicken Parmesan

Serves 4
Hands-on time: 20 min
Total time: 50 min

## Ingredients:

- 3 to 4 medium tomatoes, cut into wedges
- 3 tablespoons extra-virgin olive oil, divided
- 1/4 teaspoon kosher salt (optional)
- 1 pound chicken breast cutlets or tenders
- 1/2 cup whole-wheat panko breadcrumbs
- 1/2 cup grated Parmesan cheese, divided
- 2 tablespoons ground flaxseed
- 1/2 teaspoon paprika
- 1/2 teaspoon garlic powder
- 1/2 teaspoon ground mustard
- 1/4 teaspoon freshly ground black pepper

## Method:

1. Preheat the oven to 400°F.
2. Scatter the tomatoes on a rimmed baking sheet, and drizzle with 1 tablespoon of oil. Sprinkle with salt (if using), and slide them into the oven so they can get a head start on roasting.
3. Meanwhile, line a second baking sheet with parchment paper. Line up the chicken pieces on it, and rub with 1 tablespoon of oil.
4. In a medium bowl, mix the panko, 1/4 cup of Parmesan, flaxseed, paprika, garlic powder, ground mustard, and black pepper. Spread over the chicken. Drizzle the remaining 1 tablespoon of oil over the top.
5. Bake until the chicken is cooked through, about 20 minutes. Start checking after 15 minutes so you don't overcook it. It should be opaque with mostly clear juices. When the chicken is done, the tomatoes should be starting to brown.
6. Serve the chicken topped with the tomatoes and the remaining 1/4 cup of Parmesan cheese.

## Nutritional Content:

- Calories: 343
- Fats: 18g

- Cholesterol: 91mg
- Sodium: 370mg
- Carbohydrates: 14g

- Fiber: 3g
- Protein: 32g

# Pan-Seared Chicken

Serves 4
Hands-on time: 10min
Total time: 20min

**Ingredients:**

- 1 pound boneless, skinless chicken breasts
- 1/4 teaspoon kosher salt
- Freshly ground black pepper
- 2 tablespoons canola or sunflower oil

**Method:**

1. Pat the chicken dry with paper towels. Season with the salt and pepper.
2. Heat a large, heavy skillet over medium-high heat. Add the canola or sunflower oil. When the oil is hot (a drop of water should sizzle), add the chicken-make sure there is oil under each piece. Cover the pan.
3. After 5 minutes, check that the undersides are crispy and golden, and flip them over. If they feel stuck, give them another minute or two.
4. Cover and cook the other side for 5 minutes more, without disturbing the chicken. Use a meat thermometer to ensure that it has reached 165°F inside. It should be opaque with mostly clear juices. Transfer the chicken to a cutting board. Let it rest for a few minutes before slicing.

**Nutritional Content:**

- Calories: 198
- Fats: 10g
- Cholesterol: 1mg
- Sodium: 171mg
- Carbohydrates: 0g
- Fiber: 0g
- Protein: 26g

# Pesto, Asparagus, And Chicken Pasta

Serves 4
Hands-on time: 15 min
Total time: 15 min

**Ingredients:**

- 8 ounces uncooked bowtie pasta
- 1 pound asparagus
- 1 tablespoon extra-virgin olive oil
- 12 ounces boneless, skinless chicken breasts, cut into bite-size pieces
- 1/2 cup Walnut Pesto
- 2 medium ripe tomatoes, chopped
- 1/4 cup grated Parmesan cheese (optional)

**Method:**

1. Start cooking the pasta, setting a timer for 4 minutes less than the al dente cooking time printed on the package. Remove the woody ends of the asparagus, and cut the spears into 1 -inch pieces. When the timer goes off, scoop out 1/2 cup of cooking water and add the asparagus to the pasta pot. Bring the water back to a boil, and set the timer for 4 more minutes.
2. Meanwhile, heat the oil in a large skillet over medium-high heat. Sauté the chicken until it's cooked through, 5 to 10 minutes. It should be opaque with mostly clear juices. Stir in the tomatoes, and remove the skillet from the heat.
3. Drain the pasta and asparagus, and return them to the pasta pot. Toss with the pesto and 1/4 cup of the reserved cooking water. Add the chicken, tomatoes, and more cooking water if it seems dry. Top with the Parmesan, if desired.

**Nutritional Content:**

- Calories: 485
- Fats: 17g
- Cholesterol: 68mg
- Sodium: 201mg
- Carbohydrates: 50g
- Fiber: 5g
- Protein: 33g

# Sun-Dried Tomato Turkey Burgers

Serves 6
Hands-on time: 30 min
Total time: 30 min

## Ingredients:

- 1 pound ground turkey
- 1/2 cup rolled oats
- 1/4 cup sun-dried tomatoes in oil, drained and chopped
- 1/4 cup finely chopped red onion
- 1/4 cup chopped fresh cilantro
- 2 garlic cloves, minced
- 6 whole-wheat hamburger buns
- 1 avocado, peeled, pitted, and sliced
- 6 lettuce leaves (optional)
- 6 tomato slices (optional)

## Method:

1. Set an oven rack about 3 inches from the broiler, and preheat the broiler. Line a rimmed baking sheet with aluminum foil.
2. In a large bowl, mix the turkey with the oats, sun-dried tomatoes, onion, cilantro, and garlic. Shape into 6(1/2-inch-thick) patties.
3. Place the patties on the baking sheet, and broil for 3 to 4 minutes on each side. If you want to be sure they're done, slide an instant-read thermometer into the side of a burger. It should read 165°F.
4. While the burgers are cooking, prepare a serving platter with the buns, avocado, lettuce, and tomato (if using). Let people assemble their own burgers.

## Nutritional Content:

- Calories: 366
- Fats: 15g
- Cholesterol: 52mg
- Sodium: 353mg
- Carbohydrates: 35g
- Fiber: 6g
- Protein: 24g

# Chili Chicken, Peppers, And Corn

Serves 4
Hands-on time: 30 min
Total time: 30 min

## Ingredients:

- 3/4 cup uncooked parboiled brown rice
- 2 tablespoons canola or sunflower oil, divided
- 5 cups frozen sliced bell peppers and onions
- 1/4 teaspoon kosher salt (optional)
- Freshly ground black pepper (optional)
- 12 ounces boneless, skinless chicken breasts, cut into bite-size pieces
- 1½ cups reduced-sodium chicken broth
- 1/3 cup natural peanut butter (smooth or crunchy)
- 2 tablespoons chili powder
- 1 teaspoon dried tarragon
- 1 cup frozen corn kernels
- Juice of 1 lime (about 2 tablespoons)
- 1/2 cup chopped fresh cilantro

## Method:

1. Cook the rice according to the package directions.
2. Meanwhile, heat 1 tablespoon of oil in a large skillet over medium-high heat. When it is hot, add the peppers and onions. Sprinkle with salt and pepper (if using). Cook, stirring frequently, until they soften, 3 to 4 minutes. Transfer to a plate.
3. Add the remaining 1 tablespoon of oil and the chicken to the skillet. Sauté until the chicken is cooked through, 5 to 10 minutes. It should be opaque with mostly clear juices. Transfer to the plate with the vegetables.
4. Add the chicken broth, peanut butter, chili powder, and tarragon to the pan, stirring to mix. When the sauce comes together, add the corn. When it is hot, mix the chicken and vegetables back in.
5. Remove from the heat, and stir in the lime juice and cilantro. Serve over the rice.

## Nutritional Content:

- Calories: 521
- Fats: 22g

- Cholesterol: 64mg
- Sodium: 213mg
- Carbohydrates: 54g

- Fiber: 7g
- Protein: 31g

# Asian Chicken Lettuce Wraps

Dairy-free
Prep time: 5 minutes, plus 1 hour marinating time
Cook time: 20 minutes

**Ingredients:**

- 1/2 tablespoon olive oil
- 1/2 tablespoon dark sesame oil
- 1/2 tablespoon rice vinegar
- 1/2 tablespoon low-sodium soy sauce
- 1 teaspoon chili sauce (such as sriracha)
- 1 teaspoon peeled and grated fresh ginger
- 1/2 teaspoon freshly grated lime zest
- 1 garlic clove, minced
- 2 (6-ounce) skinless, boneless chicken breasts
- Olive oil nonstick cooking spray
- 4 Boston lettuce leaves
- 1/2 cup fresh mint leaves
- 1/2 cup bean sprouts
- 1/2 cup sliced red bell pepper
- 2 tablespoons chopped peanuts
- 1 lime, cut into 4 wedges

**Method:**

1. In a small bowl, whisk together the olive oil and sesame oil, vinegar, soy sauce, chili sauce, ginger, lime zest, and garlic. Reserve 1 tablespoon of the mixture. Add the remaining mixture to a large resealable bag. Add the chicken breasts, seal the bag, and marinate in the refrigerator for 1 hour, turning occasionally. Remove the chicken from the bag and discard the marinade.
2. Heat a large nonstick grill pan over medium- high heat. Coat the pan with cooking spray. Add the chicken and grill for about 12 minutes, or until an instant-read thermometer registers
3. 165°F, turning once halfway through. Let it stand for 5 minutes before thinly slicing.
4. Divide the chicken among the lettuce leaves. Top each lettuce leaf with mint, sprouts, bell pepper, and 1/2 teaspoon of the reserved dressing. Garnish with the chopped peanuts, wrap like a burrito, and serve with the lime wedges.

**Nutritional Content:**

- Calories: 346
- Fats: 14g

- Protein: 45g
- Cholesterol: 97mg
- Carbohydrates: 11g

- Fiber: 3g
- Sodium: 415mg

# Roasted Tomato And Chicken Pasta

Serves 4
Hands-on time: 20 min
Total time: 30 min

## Ingredients:

- 1 pound boneless, skinless chicken thighs, cut into bite-size pieces
- 1/8 teaspoon kosher salt (optional)
- 1/4 teaspoon freshly ground black pepper (optional)
- 4 cups cherry tomatoes, halved
- 4 garlic cloves, minced
- 1 tablespoon canola or sunflower oil
- 1 teaspoon dried basil
- 8 ounces uncooked whole-wheat rotini
- 10 kalamata olives, pitted and sliced
- 1/4 teaspoon red pepper flakes (optional)
- 1/4 cup grated Parmesan cheese (optional)

## Method:

1. Preheat the oven to 450°F.
2. Season the chicken with salt and pepper, if desired. Toss the chicken in a large bowl with the tomatoes, garlic, oil, and basil. Transfer to a rimmed baking sheet, and spread out evenly.
3. Roast until the chicken is cooked through, 15 to 20 minutes, tossing halfway though. A meat thermometer should read 165°F.
4. Meanwhile, cook the pasta to al dente according to the package directions. Drain.
5. In a large serving bowl, toss the chicken and tomatoes with the pasta, olives, and pepper flakes (if using). Top with Parmesan, if desired.

## Nutritional Content:

- Calories: 458
- Fats: 14g
- Cholesterol: 110mg
- Sodium: 441mg
- Carbohydrates: 52g
- Fiber: 8g
- Protein: 34g

# Oat Risotto With Mushrooms, Kale, And Chicken

Serves 4
Hands-on time: 30 min
Total time: 30min

**Ingredients:**

- 4 cups reduced-sodium chicken broth
- 1 tablespoon extra-virgin olive oil
- 1 small onion, finely chopped
- 1 pound sliced mushrooms
- 1 pound boneless, skinless chicken thighs, cut into bite-size pieces
- 1¼ cups quick-cooking steel-cut oats
- 1 (10-ounce) package frozen chopped kale (about 4 cups)
- 1/2 cup grated Parmesan cheese (optional)
- Freshly ground black pepper (optional)

**Method:**

1. In a medium saucepan, bring the broth to a simmer over medium-low heat.
2. Warm the olive oil in a large, nonstick skillet over medium-high heat. Sauté the onion and mushrooms until the onion is translucent, about 5 minutes. Push the vegetables to the side, and add the chicken. Let it sit untouched until it browns, about 2 minutes.
3. Add the oats. Cook for 1 minute, stirring constantly. Add 1/2 cup of the hot broth, and stir until it is completely absorbed. Continue stirring in broth, 1/2 cup at a time, until it is absorbed and the oats and chicken are cooked, about 10 minutes. If you run out of broth, switch to hot water.
4. Stir in the frozen kale, and cook until it's warm. Top with Parmesan and black pepper, if you like.

**Nutritional Content:**

- Calories: 470
- Fats: 16g
- Cholesterol: 118mg
- Sodium: 389mg
- Carbohydrates: 44g
- Fiber: 9g
- Protein: 40g

# Arugula Pasta Salad With Chicken

Serves 4
Hands-on time: 15 min
Total time: 15 min

**Ingredients:**

- 8 ounces uncooked whole-wheat penne
- 2 cups chopped cooked chicken
- 1 (5-ounce) package arugula, trimmed of large stems and torn into bite-size pieces if necessary
- 1/2 cup sliced Simple Roasted Peppers or jarred roasted red peppers
- 2 tablespoons extra-virgin olive oil
- Zest and juice of 1 lemon (about 3 tablespoons juice)
- 1/3 cup grated Parmesan cheese
- Freshly ground black pepper (optional)

**Method:**

1. Cook the pasta to al dente according to the package directions. When it's finished, drain and rinse with cool water.
2. Meanwhile, mix the chicken, arugula, roasted peppers, oil, and lemon zest and juice in a large salad bowl.
3. Add the pasta and toss gently to combine. Top with the cheese and black pepper, if you like.

**Nutritional Content:**

- Calories: 433
- Fats: 18g
- Cholesterol: 15mg
- Sodium: 236mg
- Carbohydrates: 46g
- Fiber: 7g
- Protein: 26g

# Chicken With Mushroom Sauce

Dairy-free, quick & easy
Prep time: 5 minutes
Cook time: 15 minutes

## Ingredients:

- 1 tablespoon olive oil, divided
- 2 (6-ounce) skinless, boneless chicken breasts
- 1/4 teaspoon salt, divided
- 1/8 teaspoon freshly ground black pepper
- 1/4 cup chopped shallots
- 4 ounces button mushrooms, sliced
- 1 portobello mushroom, sliced
- 2 garlic cloves, minced
- 1/4 cup dry white wine, cooking wine, or low-sodium broth
- 1 teaspoon flour
- 1/2 cup water
- 2 teaspoons minced fresh thyme

## Method:

1. Heat 1 teaspoon of olive oil in a large nonstick skillet over medium-high heat, swirling to coat. Sprinkle the chicken with 1/8 teaspoon salt and the pepper. Add the chicken to the skillet and cook for about 3 minutes on each side, or until an instant-read thermometer registers 165°F. Transfer the chicken to a serving platter and keep warm.
2. Add the shallots and mushrooms to the skillet and sauté, stirring occasionally, for about 4 minutes, or until browned. Add the garlic and sauté for 1 minute, stirring constantly. Add the wine and stir, scraping the pan to loosen any browned bits from the bottom. Bring to a boil and cook until the liquid almost evaporates.
3. Sprinkle the mushroom mixture with the remaining 1/8 teaspoon of salt and the flour and cook for about 30 seconds, stirring constantly. Add the water to the skillet and bring to a boil. Cook for 2 minutes more, or until slightly thick. Remove the skillet from the heat, add the remaining 2 teaspoons of olive oil and the thyme, and stir until combined.
4. Serve the sauce over the chicken.

## Nutritional Content:

- Calories: 329
- Fats: 10g
- Protein: 44g
- Cholesterol: 97mg

- Carbohydrates: 12g
- Fiber: 2g
- Sodium: 414mg

# Moroccan Spiced Chicken with Sweet Onions

Dairy-free, gluten-free
Prep time: 5 minutes, plus 10 minutes marinating time
Cook time: 20 minutes

**Ingredients:**

- 1 teaspoon ground cinnamon
- 1 teaspoon paprika
- 3/4 teaspoon ground cumin
- 1/2 teaspoon ground cardamom
- 1/2 teaspoon ground coriander
- 1/2 teaspoon ground ginger
- 1/2 teaspoon ground turmeric

- 1 tablespoon olive oil, divided
- 2 (6-ounce) skinless, boneless chicken breasts
- 1/8 teaspoon salt
- Olive oil nonstick cooking spray
- 1 cup sliced yellow onion
- 1 teaspoon honey

**Method:**

1. In small bowl, mix together the cinnamon, paprika, cumin, cardamom, coriander, ginger, and turmeric.
2. Heat 1/2 tablespoon of olive oil in a large ovenproof skillet over medium-low heat, swirling to coat. Add the spice mixture to the skillet and cook, stirring frequently, for about 3 minutes, or until toasted. In a large resealable bag, combine the spice mixture and chicken breasts, seal, and shake well to coat the chicken. Marinate the chicken in the refrigerator for 10 minutes.
3. Preheat the oven to 350°F.
4. Remove the chicken from the bag and sprinkle with the salt. Heat the skillet over medium-high heat and lightly coat it with cooking spray. Add the chicken and cook for about 4 minutes. Turn the chicken over and cook for 1 minute more. Remove the chicken from the pan.
5. Add the remaining 1/2 tablespoon of olive oil to the pan, swirling to coat. Add the onion and sauté for 2 minutes, or until it starts to brown. Return the chicken to the pan and drizzle the
6. honey over all.
7. Bake for 10 minutes, or until an instant-read thermometer registers 165°F. Serve immediately.

**Nutritional Content:**

- Calories: 295
- Fats: 10g
- Protein: 40g
- Cholesterol: 97mg

- Carbohydrates: 11g
- Fiber: 3g
- Sodium: 261mg

# Chapter 6: Seafood

## Tuna, Cashew, And Couscous Salad

Serves 3
Hands-on time: 15 min
Total time: 15 min

### Ingredients:

- 1/2 cup uncooked whole-wheat couscous
- 1/4 teaspoon salt
- 1 (5-ounce) can sustainably sourced tuna, packed in oil
- 1 bell pepper, any color, seeded and chopped
- 1 (12-ounce) package broccoli slaw (about 4 cups)
- 3 scallions, finely chopped
- 3 tablespoons red wine vinegar
- 2 tablespoons extra-virgin olive oil
- 1 teaspoon dried oregano
- 1 teaspoon dried thyme
- 1/2 teaspoon freshly ground black pepper
- 1/2 cup chopped unsalted roasted cashews

### Method:

1. Prepare the couscous with the salt, according to the package directions. Transfer to a medium bowl, and let it cool until the other ingredients are ready.
2. Drain the tuna, and use a fork to mash it well in a large bowl. Add the bell pepper, broccoli slaw, scallions, vinegar, oil, oregano, thyme, and black pepper.
3. Add the couscous, and toss well. Adjust the seasonings, if desired. Top with the cashews.

### Nutritional Content:

- Calories: 457
- Fats: 24g
- Cholesterol: 15mg
- Sodium: 450mg
- Carbohydrates: 39g
- Fiber: 6g
- Protein: 24g

# Spicy Shrimp, Feta, And Walnut Couscous

Serves 4
Hands-on time: 25 min
Total time: 30 min

**Ingredients:**

- 1 tablespoon extra-virgin olive oil
- 2 cups frozen sliced onions and bell peppers
- 2 medium ripe tomatoes, chopped
- 2 garlic cloves, minced
- 1½ cups reduced-sodium chicken broth
- 1/2 teaspoon cayenne pepper
- 12 ounces sustainably sourced, frozen raw shrimp, thawed and peeled
- 1 cup uncooked whole-wheat couscous
- 1/3 cup chopped walnuts
- 1/3 cup crumbled feta cheese

**Method:**

1. Heat the oil in a large, heavy skillet over medium-high heat. When the oil is hot, add the onions and peppers. Cook, stirring occasionally, for 3 to 4 minutes.
2. Add the tomato and garlic, and cook for 1 minute. Add the chicken broth and cayenne pepper, and bring to a boil. Add the shrimp, and return to a boil.
3. Stir in the couscous. Remove the skillet from the heat, cover, and let stand until the couscous is tender and all the broth is absorbed, about 5 minutes.
4. Fluff with a fork. Top with the walnuts and feta cheese.

**Nutritional Content:**

- Calories: 392
- Fats: 14g
- Cholesterol: 150mg
- Sodium: 490mg
- Carbohydrates: 40g
- Fiber: 5g
- Protein: 29g

# Pan-Seared Halibut With Chimichurri

Serves 4
Hands-on time: 10 min
Total time: 10 min

**Ingredients:**

- 2 tablespoons extra-virgin olive oil
- 4 (5- to 6-ounce) sustainably sourced halibut fillets, fresh or thawed
- 1 recipe Chimichurri

**Method:**

1. Heat the oil in a large, nonstick skillet over medium-high heat. When the oil is hot, sear the halibut for about 5 minutes on each side, until it flakes easily and is cooked to an internal temperature of 145°F.
2. Serve immediately, topped with the Chimichurri.

**Nutritional Content:**

- Calories: 371
- Fats: 25g
- Cholesterol: 112mg
- Sodium: 248mg
- Carbohydrates: 5g
- Fiber: 1g
- Protein: 32g

# Open-Faced Lemon Pepper Tuna Melt

Serves 2
Hands-on time: 15 min
Total time: 15 min

## Ingredients:

- 2 teaspoons Better Butter or nonhydrogenated margarine
- 2 slices sprouted-grain bread
- 1 (5-ounce) can sustainably sourced tuna, packed in water
- 2 teaspoons extra-virgin olive oil
- 2 teaspoons mayonnaise
- 1 teaspoon lemon zest
- 1 tablespoon freshly squeezed lemon juice
- 2 tablespoons finely chopped red onion (optional)
- 1/2 teaspoon red pepper flakes (optional)
- Freshly ground black pepper
- 1/4 cup shredded Cheddar cheese

## Method:

1. Set the oven rack about 6 inches from the heat, and preheat the broiler.
2. Spread butter thinly on both sides of bread. Place the bread on a rimmed baking sheet. Toast the bread under the broiler untilit is golden brown on both sides, about 2 minutes on each side. Watch it carefully to make sure it doesn't burn.
3. Drain the tuna well, and mash in a medium bowl with the oil, mayonnaise, lemon zest and juice, red onion and red pepper flakes (if using), and black pepper. Mix well.
4. Divide the tuna mixture between the two slices of bread, making sure the bread is completely covered. Sprinkle with the cheese.
5. Broil until the cheese is melted, 2 to 3 minutes.

## Nutritional Content:

- Calories: 336
- Fats: 19g
- Cholesterol: 46mg
- Sodium: 450mg
- Carbohydrates: 21g
- Fiber: 4g
- Protein: 22g

# Pecan-Crusted Catfish With Roasted Romaine

Serves 4
Hands-on time: 20 min
Total time: 30 min

## Ingredients:

- 2 tablespoons extra-virgin olive oil, divided
- 2 hearts of romaine, halved lengthwise
- 1 garlic clove, minced
- 1/2 cup all-purpose flour
- 1 large egg
- 2 tablespoons water
- 1/4 teaspoon paprika
- 1/2 cup very finely chopped pecans
- 12 ounces sustainably sourced catfish fillets, fresh or thawed
- 1/4 teaspoon kosher salt
- Freshly ground black pepper
- 1 lemon, cut into wedges

## Method:

1. Preheat the oven to 425°F. Line two rimmed baking sheets with parchment paper, and drizzle each with 1/2 tablespoon of oil.
2. Lay the romaine halves, cut-side up, on one sheet, and drizzle with the remaining 1 tablespoon of oil. Sprinkle the romaine with the garlic.
3. Set the other sheet next to three wide bowls. Fill one bowl with the flour, beat the egg, water, and paprika together in the second bowl, and fill the last bowl with the pecans.
4. Pat the fish dry with a paper towel. Sprinkle with salt and pepper. Dip and flip each fillet in the flour, then the egg mixture, then the pecans. Lay on the baking sheet. Press any unused pecans into the fish.
5. Put both baking sheets in the oven and roast until the fish just starts to flake easily, 8 to 10 minutes. By then the romaine should be nicely browned. If not, remove the fish from the oven and broil the romaine for 2 to 3 minutes, watching carefully. Serve with lemon wedges.

## Nutritional Content:

- Calories: 367
- Fats: 21g
- Cholesterol: 96mg
- Sodium: 80mg
- Carbohydrates: 25g
- Fiber: 8g
- Protein: 22g

# Chili Salmon Sheet Pan Dinner

Serves 4
Hands-on time: 20 min
Total time: 30 min

## Ingredients:

- 1½ tablespoons chili powder
- 1/2 teaspoon dried oregano
- 1/4 teaspoon kosher salt
- 1 large sweet potato, scrubbed and cut into 3/4-inch cubes
- 2 tablespoons canola or sunflower oil, divided
- 1 head broccoli, cut into florets, or 2 cups frozen broccoli florets
- 1 pound sustainably sourced salmon fillets, fresh or thawed

## Method:

1. Preheat the oven to 420°F. Line two rimmed baking sheets with parchment paper.
2. Mix the chili powder, oregano, and salt in a small bowl.
3. Toss the sweet potato in a large bowl with 1 tablespoon of oil and 1 teaspoon of seasoning mix. Spread out on one baking sheet, and slide into the oven.
4. In the same bowl, toss the broccoli with the remaining 1 tablespoon of oil and another 1 teaspoon of seasoning. Spread out on the other baking sheet, and put in the oven. Set a timer for 5 minutes.
5. Rub the remainder of the seasoning mix onto the salmon. When the timer goes off, toss the sweet potatoes and broccoli. Slide them over, and add the salmon to the sheet pans.
6. Remove the salmon from the sheet pans when it is nearly done (see Cooking Tip), 8 to 10 minutes, depending on thickness, and tent with foil. Keep roasting the vegetables until they are as crisp as you like them, about 5 minutes more.

## Nutritional Content:

- Calories: 317
- Fats: 14g
- Cholesterol: 62mg
- Sodium: 233mg
- Carbohydrates: 21g
- Fiber: 4g
- Protein: 25g

# Electric Chickpeas And Shrimp

Serves 3
Hands-on time: 20 min
Total time: 20 min

**Ingredients:**

- 7 ounces sustainably sourced, frozen cooked shrimp, thawed and peeled
- 1 (15-ounce) can no-salt-added chickpeas, rinsed and drained
- 1 red bell pepper, seeded and diced
- 1/3 cup finely chopped red onion
- 1 garlic clove, finely chopped
- 1/2 cup red wine vinegar
- 3 tablespoons extra-virgin olive oil
- 1/2 teaspoon paprika
- 1/2 teaspoon dried oregano
- 1/8 teaspoon salt
- Pinch cayenne pepper

**Method:**

1. Toss together the shrimp, chickpeas, bell pepper, onion, garlic, vinegar, olive oil, paprika, oregano, salt, and cayenne pepper in a large bowl. Taste, and adjust the seasonings.

**Nutritional Content:**

- Calories: 338
- Fats: 15g
- Cholesterol: 83mg
- Sodium: 510mg
- Carbohydrates: 28g
- Fiber: 7g
- Protein: 17g

# Rosemary-Lemon Salmon

Serves 4
Hands-on time: 10 min
Total time: 25 min

**Ingredients:**

- 1 pound sustainably sourced fresh, skin-on salmon fillets
- Zest and juice of 1/2 lemon (about 1½ tablespoons juice)
- 1 garlic clove, minced
- 1/4 teaspoon kosher salt
- Freshly ground black pepper
- 2 fresh rosemary sprigs or 1 teaspoon dried rosemary
- 1 tablespoon extra-virgin olive oil (optional)

**Method:**

1. Set the oven rack to the second-highest level, and preheat the broiler.
2. Line a rimmed baking sheet with aluminum foil. Place the salmon, skin-side down, on the sheet. Top with the lemon zest and juice, garlic, salt, and pepper. Lay the rosemary sprigs on top. Drizzle with olive oil (if using).
3. Broil the salmon for 5 minutes, then move to a lower rack and reduce the heat to 325°F.
4. Cook for another 8 to 10 minutes, until the salmon is nearly done (see the Cooking Tip). Let the fish rest, tented with foil, for 5 minutes before serving.

**Nutritional Content:**

- Calories: 193
- Fats: 11g
- Cholesterol: 62mg
- Sodium: 171mg
- Carbohydrates: 1g
- Fiber: 0g
- Protein: 23g

# Salmon And Scallop Skewers

Dairy-free, gluten-free
Prep time: 30 minutes, plus 1 hour marinating time
Cook time: 12 minutes

## Ingredients:

- 1 (8-ounce) can pineapple chunks in 100% pineapple juice, drained, reserving 2 tablespoons juice
- 1 tablespoon freshly squeezed lemon juice
- 1 tablespoon snipped fresh tarragon or 1 teaspoon dried tarragon
- 1/4 teaspoon dry mustard
- 1/8 teaspoon salt
- 4 ounces skinless, boneless wild salmon fillets, cut into
- 1-inch cubes
- 4 ounces scallops
- 1 zucchini, cut into 1/2-inch-thick slices
- 1 red bell pepper, cut into 1-inch squares
- 1 red onion, cut into 1-inch pieces
- 8 button mushrooms

## Method:

1. Preheat an outdoor grill.
2. In a small bowl, combine the 2 tablespoons of reserved pineapple juice, the lemon juice, tarragon, mustard, and salt. Place the salmon and scallops in a resealable bag, add the marinade and seal the bag. Turn the fish and scallops to coat well. Marinate in the refrigerator for 1 to 2 hours, turning once.
3. Meanwhile, in a small saucepan, bring just enough water to cover the zucchini (1 to 2 inches) to a boil. Add the zucchini and cook, covered, for 3 to 4 minutes, or until nearly tender. Drain and cool.
4. Remove the seafood from the bag, reserving the marinade. On 4 metal skewers, alternately thread the salmon, scallops, zucchini, bell pepper, onion, mushrooms, and pineapple. Brush with the reserved marinade.
5. Grill, uncovered, directly over medium coals for 8 to 12 minutes, turning once, until the scallops turn opaque and the salmon flakes easily when tested with a fork.
6. Serve two skewers on each dinner plate.

## Nutritional Content:

- Calories: 260
- Fats: 5g
- Protein: 26g
- Cholesterol: 44mg

- Carbohydrates: 32g
- Fiber: 6g
- Sodium: 285mg

# Sesame-Crusted Tuna Steaks

Dairy-free, gluten-free, quick & easy
Prep time: 5 minutes
Cook time: 12 minutes

**Ingredients:**

- Olive oil nonstick cooking spray
- 1/2 tablespoon olive oil
- 1 teaspoon sesame oil
- 2 (6-ounce) ahi tuna steaks
- 6 tablespoons sesame seeds
- Salt
- Freshly ground black pepper

**Method:**

1. Preheat the oven to 450°F and lightly spray a baking sheet with cooking spray.
2. In a small bowl, stir together the olive oil and sesame oil. Brush the tuna steaks with the oil mixture.
3. Put the sesame seeds in a shallow bowl. Press the steaks into the seeds, turning to cover all sides.
4. Place the tuna steaks on the prepared baking sheet. Sprinkle with salt and pepper. Bake for 4 to 6 minutes per 1/2-inch thickness of fish, or until the fish begins to flake when tested with a fork. Serve immediately.

**Nutritional Content:**

- Calories: 520
- Fats: 30g
- Protein: 56g
- Cholesterol: 83mg
- Carbohydrates: 6g
- Fiber: 3g
- Sodium: 166mg

# Tomato And Zucchini With Salmon And Farro

Serves 4
Hands-on time: 25 min
Total time: 25 min

**Ingredients:**

- 1 cup uncooked farro
- 2 tablespoons extra-virgin olive oil
- 4 shallots, thinly sliced
- 2 cups cherry tomatoes, halved
- 1 teaspoon dried thyme
- 1 medium zucchini
- 2 garlic cloves
- Zest and juice of 1 lemon (about 3 tablespoons juice)
- 1 (7.5-ounce) can wild salmon, drained
- 4 cups baby spinach
- 1/2 cup crumbled feta cheese

**Method:**

1. Cook the farro according to the package directions.
2. Meanwhile, heat the oil in a large skillet over medium heat. Add the shallots, tomatoes, and thyme. Cook until the shallots start to brown, 5 or 6 minutes.
3. While that's cooking, grate or spiralize the zucchini and mince the garlic.
4. Add the zucchini, garlic, and lemon zest and juice to the skillet with the tomatoes, and cook for a few minutes, stirring occasionally.
5. Drain the salmon, reserving 1 tablespoon of the liquid from the can. Add the salmon to the skillet, along with the reserved canning liquid. Break the fish apart with a fork. Add the cooked farro and the spinach. Stir everything together to heat through.
6. Taste and adjust the seasonings. Top with the feta cheese.

**Nutritional Content:**

- Calories: 405
- Fats: 15g
- Cholesterol: 52mg
- Sodium: 411mg
- Carbohydrates: 43g
- Fiber: 7g
- Protein: 26g

# Lemon Garlic Mackerel

Dairy-free, gluten-free, quick & easy
Prep time: 10 minutes
Cook time: 5 minutes

**Ingredients:**

- 2 (4-ounce) mackerel fillets
- Salt
- 2 garlic cloves, minced
- Juice of 1/2 lemon
- Freshly ground black pepper

**Method:**

1. Line a baking sheet with aluminum foil and lay the fillets on it. Sprinkle them with salt and leave them for 5 minutes. This helps give the fish a firmer texture.
2. Meanwhile, preheat the broiler.
3. In a small bowl, mix together the garlic, lemon juice, and some pepper. Pour the mixture over the mackerel.
4. Broil for about 5 minutes, or until the fish is opaque and flakes easily with a fork. Serve immediately.

**Nutritional Content:**

- Calories: 302
- Fats: 20g
- Protein: 27g
- Cholesterol: 85mg
- Carbohydrates: 1g
- Fiber: 0g
- Sodium: 172mg

# Salmon And Summer Squash In Parchment

Dairy-free, gluten-free
Prep time: 15 minutes
Cook time: 17 minutes

**Ingredients:**

- 2 tablespoons freshly squeezed lemon juice
- 1 cup sliced yellow summer squash
- 2 tablespoons sliced shallot
- 1 tablespoon chopped fresh oregano leaves
- 1/2 tablespoon olive oil
- 1/8 teaspoon salt
- 1/8 teaspoon freshly ground black pepper
- 1 cup sliced medium zucchini
- 2 (6-ounce) skinless salmon fillets
- 1 teaspoon grated lemon zest, divided

**Method:**

1. Preheat the oven to 400°F.
2. In a medium bowl, combine the lemon juice, yellow squash, shallot, oregano, olive oil, salt, and pepper.
3. Place 2 large parchment rectangles on the work surface with the short side of the parchment closest to you. On half of one parchment rectangle, arrange half the zucchini slices lengthwise, overlapping them slightly. Place a salmon fillet on the zucchini, sprinkle with half the lemon zest, then top with half the yellow squash mixture. Fold the parchment over the ingredients. Repeat with the other piece of parchment and the remaining ingredients. To seal the packets, begin at one corner and tightly fold over the edges about 1/2 inch all around, overlapping the folds.
4. Place the packets on a baking sheet and bake for about 17 minutes, or until the salmon turns opaque throughout.
5. To serve, carefully cut the packets open, being careful to avoid escaping steam, and with a spatula gently transfer the salmon and vegetables to two plates. Spoon any liquid remaining in the parchment over the salmon and vegetables.

**Nutritional Content:**

- Calories: 291
- Fats: 15g
- Protein: 35g
- Cholesterol: 75mg
- Carbohydrates: 7g
- Fiber: 2g
- Sodium: 238mg

# Spicy Salmon Sandwiches

Serves 4
Hands-on time: 15 min
Total time: 15 min

## Ingredients:

- 1 (6-ounce) can wild salmon, drained
- 2 tablespoons mayonnaise
- 1/4 teaspoon Sriracha sauce
- 1/4 teaspoon dried dill
- 1/2 cup shredded carrot
- 1/2 cup finely diced celery
- 1/2 cup canned, no-salt-added chickpeas, rinsed and drained
- 1/4 cup unsalted sunflower seeds
- 8 slices sprouted-grain bread, toasted
- 4 lettuce leaves

## Method:

1. In a medium bowl, mash the salmon together with the mayonnaise, Sriracha, and dill. Mix in the carrot, celery, chickpeas, and sunflower seeds.
2. Spread the salmon onto 4 slices of toast. Top with the lettuce and the other slices of toast.

## Nutritional Content:

- Calories: 409
- Fats: 14g
- Cholesterol: 36mg
- Sodium: 548mg
- Carbohydrates: 47g
- Fiber: 10g
- Protein: 24g

# Flounder Tacos With Cabbage Slaw

Dairy-free, gluten-free, quick & easy
Prep time: 10 minutes
Cook time: 6 minutes

**Ingredients:**

- 8 ounces skinless flounder fillets, cut into 1-inch chunks
- 1 teaspoon ground cumin
- 1/8 teaspoon salt
- 1/8 teaspoon freshly ground black pepper
- 1 cup thinly sliced red cabbage
- 1/2 avocado, chopped
- 2 tablespoons freshly squeezed lime juice
- 3 teaspoons olive oil, divided
- 4 corn tortillas, warmed
- Fresh cilantro, for garnish

**Method:**

1. In a small bowl, mix together the flounder, cumin, salt, and pepper.
2. In another small bowl, mix together the cabbage, avocado, lime juice, and 1 teaspoon of olive oil.
3. Heat the remaining 2 teaspoons of olive oil in a medium-size skillet over medium-high heat. Add the flounder to the skillet and cook, turning, for about 4 minutes, or until the fish is just opaque and flakes easily with a fork.
4. Place 2 warm tortillas on each serving plate. Divide the fish among the tortillas and top with the cabbage-avocado slaw. Serve garnished with fresh cilantro.

**Nutritional Content:**

- Calories: 413
- Fats: 20g
- Protein: 32g
- Cholesterol: 77mg
- Carbohydrates: 28g
- Fiber: 7g
- Sodium: 299mg

# Chapter 7: Meat

## Steak with Onions and Peppers

Dairy-free, gluten-free, quick & easy
Prep time: 5 minutes
Cook time: 12 minutes

**Ingredients:**

- 8 ounces top round steak, cut into thin strips
- Salt
- Freshly ground black pepper
- Olive oil nonstick cooking spray
- 1/2 large white onion, cut into rings
- 1 small green bell pepper, cut into big chunks
- 1 small red bell pepper, cut into big chunks
- 2 teaspoons crushed garlic
- 1/2 teaspoon olive oil
- 1/2 cup sliced mushrooms

**Method:**

1. Season steak with salt and pepper.
2. Heat a large skillet over high heat and spray it with cooking spray.
3. Add half the steak, cook for 1 minute, turn the strips over, and cook for 30 seconds more. Transfer the strips to a large dish.
4. Spray the skillet with cooking spray again. Add the remaining steak, cook for 1 minute, turn the strips over, and cook for 30 seconds more. Add to the dish with the cooked steak strips.
5. Return the skillet to the heat and spray with cooking spray again. Add the onion, bell peppers, and garlic and season with salt and pepper. Cook for 3 to 4 minutes, or until the onions are golden and the peppers are soft. Add the cooked vegetables to the dish with the steak.
6. Decrease the heat to medium and add the olive oil to the skillet. Add the mushrooms and cook for about 4 minutes.
7. Add the mushrooms to the dish with the steak, onions, and peppers and stir to combine. Serve immediately.

**Nutritional Content:**

- Calories: 285
- Fats: 7g

- Protein: 43g
- Cholesterol: 102mg
- Carbohydrates: 11g

- Fiber: 3g
- Sodium: 134mg

# Red Onions Stuffed With Grilled Steak And Spinach

Dairy-free, gluten-free
Prep time: 10 minutes
Cook time: 55 minutes

**Ingredients:**

- 2 (15-to 16-ounce) red onions, peeled and tops removed
- 1 tablespoon olive oil
- 2 teaspoons minced garlic
- 2 teaspoons minced fresh ginger
- 1/2 teaspoon garam masala
- 1/2 teaspoon ground cumin
- 2 tablespoons golden raisins
- 2 tablespoons water
- 8 ounces grilled flank steak, cut into 1/2 -inch dice
- 8 ounces baby spinach, roughly chopped
- 1/2 tablespoon freshly squeezed lemon juice
- Salt
- Freshly ground black pepper

**Method:**

1. In a 4-quart pot, bring 2 quarts of water to a boil. Carefully place the onions in the boiling water and cook for 25 to 30 minutes, or until they are tender but still retain their shape. Drain and let them cool.
2. Position a rack in the center of the oven and preheat the oven to 375°F.
3. When the onions are cool enough to handle, cut them in half crosswise and trim the root ends. Holding an onion wrapped in a clean towel, use your fingers to carefully remove the core from each half of the onion, leaving a 1/2-inch thick shell. Cut a small amount off the bottom of each half so they sit upright. Repeat with the second onion. Roughly chop and reserve 1/2 cup of the removed onion core.
4. In a large skillet over medium-high heat, heat the olive oil until it shimmers. Add the garlic and ginger and cook, stirring, for about 1½ minutes, or until lightly browned. Add the garam masala and cumin and continue cooking, stirring, for about 30 seconds, or until fragrant. Decrease the heat to medium, add the raisins and water and cook for about 1 minute, or until the raisins are plump. Add the reserved chopped onion and the flank steak and cook, stirring frequently, 1 to 2 minutes, or until heated through. Add the spinach and cook, stirring, for 1 to 2 minutes, or until wilted. Add the lemon juice and season with salt and pepper.

5. Spoon the filling into the onion halves, mounding it slightly. Put the onions on a rimmed baking sheet and bake until the tops just begin to brown, about 15 minutes. Serve immediately.

**Nutritional Content:**

- Calories: 521
- Fats: 14g
- Protein: 50g
- Cholesterol: 102mg

- Carbohydrates: 53g
- Fiber: 12g
- Sodium: 239mg

# Southwest Steak Skillet

Serves 4
Hands-on time: 25 min
Total time: 25 min

## Ingredients:

- 2/3 cup uncooked quinoa
- 1 tablespoon canola or sunflower oil
- 12 ounces top sirloin beef, trimmed and thinly sliced
- 1/2 red onion, chopped
- 1 green bell pepper, seeded and chopped
- 1 cup no-salt-added black beans, rinsed and drained
- 2/3 cup reduced-sodium chicken broth
- 1 tablespoon Salt-Free Southwest Seasoning Mix or Mrs. Dash, plus more if needed
- 1 avocado, peeled, pitted, and diced
- 1/2 cup Fresh Tomato Salsa or lower-sodium store-bought salsa

## Method:

1. Cook the quinoa according to the package directions.
2. Meanwhile, heat the oil in a heavy skillet over medium-high heat. When it is hot, cook the steak slices until just cooked through, 3 to 4 minutes. Transfer to a plate.
3. Sauté the onion and pepper in the pan drippings until soft, 4 to 5 minutes. Turn the heat down to medium, if needed, to prevent them from burning. Add the black beans, broth, and Southwest seasoning. Turn the heat down to medium, cover, and cook, for 5 minutes.
4. Stir in the cooked quinoa when it is ready. Return the steak to the pan. Taste and add more Southwest Seasoning, if desired. Garnish with avocado and salsa.

## Nutritional Content:

- Calories: 440
- Fats: 22g
- Cholesterol: 59mg
- Sodium: 158mg
- Carbohydrates: 36g
- Fiber: 9g
- Protein: 26g

# Pork Chops With Tomato And Fennel Sauce

Dairy-free, gluten-free, quick & easy
Prep time: 10 minutes
Cook time: 20 minutes

## Ingredients:

- 2 teaspoons olive oil
- 1 fennel bulb, thinly sliced (2 to 3 cups)
- 2 medium shallots, thinly sliced
- 3 garlic cloves, minced
- 1 (14-ounce) can diced tomatoes, with juices
- 3/4 teaspoon dried oregano
- 1/2 teaspoon dried rosemary
- 1/4 teaspoon dried thyme
- Salt
- Freshly ground black pepper
- 1 garlic clove, peeled and halved lengthwise
- 4 (2-ounce) boneless, center-cut pork chops (about 1/4-inch thick)
- 1/4 cup chopped fresh parsley

## Method:

1. In a large nonstick skillet over medium-high heat, add the olive oil, fennel, and shallots and sauté for 4 to 5 minutes.
2. Add the garlic and cook for an additional minute. Add the tomatoes, oregano, rosemary, and thyme and season with salt and pepper. Simmer for 8 to 10 minutes.
3. About 5 minutes into the simmering time, take the garlic clove and rub both sides of the pork chops. Season the chops with salt and pepper. Cook the chops in the skillet for 3 to 4 minutes per side until an instant-read thermometer registers 145°F. Allow them to rest for 1 minute.
4. Divide the tomato-fennel mixture between two serving plates and top each with 2 pork chops. Garnish with the fresh parsley and enjoy immediately.

## Nutritional Content:

- Calories: 497
- Fats: 28g
- Protein: 30g
- Cholesterol: 98mg
- Carbohydrates: 21g
- Fiber: 7g
- Sodium: 312mg

# Smothered Pork Chops With Rosemary And Thyme

Quick & easy
Prep time: 5 minutes
Cook time: 15 minutes

**Ingredients:**

- 1/2 cup low-sodium or unsalted beef broth, divided
- 2 tablespoons nonfat milk or plant-based milk
- 2 teaspoons oat flour
- 2 teaspoons Dijon mustard
- 1/8 teaspoon salt
- 1/8 teaspoon freshly ground black pepper
- 4 (2-ounce) boneless center-cut loin pork chops (about 1/4 -inch thick)
- 1/4 teaspoon paprika
- 1/2 teaspoon dried thyme
- 1/2 teaspoon dried rosemary
- Olive oil nonstick cooking spray
- 2 garlic cloves, minced
- 1/2 cup sliced button mushrooms
- 1/2 cup chopped onion
- 1/4 cup water
- 1/4 cup white cooking wine
- 1 tablespoon minced fresh parsley, for garnish

**Method:**

1. In a small bowl, whisk together 1/4 cup of broth, the milk, flour, mustard, salt, and pepper and set it aside.
2. Sprinkle one side of each pork chop with the paprika, thyme, and rosemary. Heat a large nonstick skillet over medium-high heat. Coat the skillet with cooking spray. Add the pork chops to the skillet and sauté for about 2 minutes on each side, or until an instant- read thermometer registers 145°F. Remove the chops from the skillet.
3. Decrease the heat to medium, add the garlic, mushrooms, and onion and sauté for about 4 minutes, or until lightly golden. Add the remaining 1/4 cup of broth, the water, and wine. Bring to a boil and cook for about 2 minutes. Whisk in the reserved milk mixture. Add the pork, turning to coat, and cook for about 1 minute.
4. Transfer to two serving plates, sprinkle with the parsley, and serve warm.

**Nutritional Content:**

- Calories: 439
- Fats: 29g
- Protein: 29g
- Cholesterol: 98mg

- Carbohydrates: 8g
- Fiber: 2g
- Sodium: 234mg

# Chili-Lime Pork Tenderloin

Dairy-free
Prep time: 5 minutes, plus 1 hour marinating time
Cook time: 30 minutes

## Ingredients:

- 1 teaspoon chili powder
- 2 tablespoons freshly squeezed lime juice
- 2 tablespoons chopped fresh cilantro
- 1 teaspoon low-sodium soy sauce
- 2 garlic cloves, minced
- 1/2 teaspoon sugar
- 8 ounces pork tenderloin
- 1/2 tablespoon olive oil
- 1/2 avocado, peeled, pitted, and sliced

## Method:

1. In a small bowl, mix the chili powder, lime juice, cilantro, soy sauce, garlic, and sugar. Using your fingers, rub the mixture thoroughly onto all sides of the tenderloin. Transfer the tenderloin to a dish and refrigerate for 1 hour.
2. Preheat the oven to 400°F.
3. When the pork is marinated, heat the olive oil in a large ovenproof skillet. Add the pork and sear it on all sides, turning with tongs, about 2 minutes total.
4. Transfer the skillet to the oven and bake for 20 to 25 minutes, depending on the thickness of the tenderloin, or until an instant-read thermometer registers 145°F. Baste after about 10 minutes of cooking with any juices that have accumulated, adding 2 tablespoons of water if necessary, to prevent scorching.
5. Transfer the tenderloin to a cutting board, cover loosely with foil, and let it rest for 5 minutes. Slice on the diagonal into 1/2-inch-thick pieces and serve with the avocado slices.

## Nutritional Content:

- Calories: 309
- Fats: 18g
- Protein: 31g
- Cholesterol: 83mg
- Carbohydrates: 7g
- Fiber: 4g
- Sodium: 231mg

# Mango And Pork Stir-Fry

Serves 4
Hands-on time: 30 min
Total time: 30 min

## Ingredients:

- 1 (1-pound) boneless pork tenderloin
- 1/4 teaspoon kosher salt (optional)
- Freshly ground black pepper (optional)
- 1/3 cup sesame seeds
- 1 tablespoon canola or sunflower oil
- 2 teaspoons minced fresh ginger
- 2 garlic cloves, minced
- 1 red bell pepper, seeded and chopped
- 2 tablespoons rice vinegar
- 1½ tablespoons reduced-sodium tamari
- 2 teaspoons sesame oil
- 1 cup frozen mango chunks, any large pieces cut in half
- 1 cup snow peas, trimmed

## Method:

1. Cut the tenderloin in half lengthwise, then thinly slice each half. Season with salt and pepper (if using).
2. Heat a large, heavy skillet over medium heat. When it's hot, add the sesame seeds and toast, stirring frequently, until lightly browned, 3 to 5 minutes. Immediately transfer them to a small bowl.
3. Add the oil to the skillet. When it's hot, add the pork. Sauté until lightly browned, 3 to 5 minutes. Add the ginger and garlic, and cook for a minute more. Transfer to a plate. Add the bell pepper to the skillet and cook for 3 to 4 minutes.
4. Add the rice vinegar, tamari, and sesame oil to the bowl with the sesame seeds, and whisk until mixed. Add the sauce and mango to the skillet. Cook until the mango is warm, about 2 minutes. Add the snow peas and pork, and cook until just warmed through.

## Nutritional Content:

- Calories: 306
- Fats: 14g
- Cholesterol: 74mg
- Sodium: 451mg
- Carbohydrates: 17g
- Fiber: 5g
- Protein: 29g

# Beef And Corn Fiesta Salad

Serves 4
Hands-on time: 25 min
Total time: 25 min

## Ingredients:

- 2 cups frozen corn kernels
- 8 ounces extra-lean (7% fat) ground beef
- 1/4 teaspoon kosher salt
- Freshly ground black pepper (optional)
- 1 small onion, chopped
- 1 (15-ounce) can no-salt-added kidney beans, rinsed and drained
- 1 (14-ounce) can no-salt-added diced tomatoes
- 1 teaspoon chili powder
- 1 teaspoon ground cumin
- 4 cups torn romaine lettuce
- 2 medium tomatoes, chopped
- 1 avocado, peeled, pitted, and sliced
- 1/2 cup shredded Cheddar cheese

## Method:

1. Put the corn in a large salad bowl to let it thaw.
2. Meanwhile, place a large sauté pan over medium heat. When it's hot, add the beef. Season with salt and pepper, if desired. Do not touch for 2-3 minutes, until the bottom is nicely browned.
3. Add the onion, and continue to brown the meat, stirring to cook on all sides. When it is no longer pink, add the beans, canned tomatoes with their juice, chili powder, and cumin. Simmer for 5 minutes.
4. Add the lettuce and fresh tomatoes to the salad bowl, and toss. Add the avocado slices on one side of the salad. Add the beef mixture on the other side. Sprinkle with the cheese.

## Nutritional Content:

- Calories: 409
- Fats: 15g
- Cholesterol: 50mg
- Sodium: 292mg
- Carbohydrates: 47g
- Fiber: 17g
- Protein: 27g

# Mushroom Bolognese

Serves 6(1⅓ cups per serving)
Hands-on time: 20 min
Total time: 30 min

## Ingredients:

- 1 pound extra-lean (7% fat) ground beef
- 1/2 teaspoon salt, divided (optional)
- Freshly ground black pepper
- 1 onion, chopped
- 3 garlic cloves, minced
- 1/2 cup uncooked split red lentils, rinsed
- 1 (28-ounce) can whole, no-salt-added tomatoes
- 1 pound sliced mushrooms
- 2/3 cup water
- 2 tablespoons tomato paste
- 1 tablespoon dried oregano

## Method:

1. Heat a large sauté pan over medium heat. When the pan is hot, add the beef and sprinkle with 1/4 teaspoon salt (if using) and the pepper. Do not stir the meat until it is browned on the bottom, 2 to 3 minutes. Add the onion and garlic, and stir periodically until the beef is no longer pink, 5 to 7 minutes.
2. Turn up the heat and add the lentils, tomatoes with their juice, mushrooms, water, tomato paste, and oregano. When it boils, reduce the heat to medium and simmer, stirring occasionally, until the lentils are soft, about 15 minutes.
3. Taste, and add an extra 1/4 teaspoon of salt and pepper, if desired.

## Nutritional Content:

- Calories: 225
- Fats: 6g
- Cholesterol: 48mg
- Sodium: 266mg
- Carbohydrates: 21g
- Fiber: 5g
- Protein: 24g

# Sliced Pork Loin For Sandwiches

Serves 4
Hands-on time: 10 min
Total time: 30 min

**Ingredients:**

- 1 teaspoon onion powder
- 1/2 teaspoon garlic powder
- 1/2 teaspoon dried thyme
- 1/4 teaspoon kosher salt
- 1/4 teaspoon freshly ground black pepper
- 1 (1-pound) boneless pork tenderloin roast
- 1 tablespoon canola or sunflower oil

**Method:**

1. Preheat the oven to 425°F.
2. Mix the onion powder, garlic powder, thyme, salt, and pepper in a small bowl. Trim the tenderloin of any silverskin, and pat dry. Rub all over with the seasoning.
3. Heat the oil in a large, oven-safe skillet over medium-high heat. (If you don't have an oven-safe skillet, use a regular skillet and place an aluminum foil-lined roasting pan in the oven to heat up.) When the skillet is very hot, sear the pork for 2 minutes on each side. Transfer the skillet to the oven (or transfer the steak to the roasting pan).
4. Cook until the internal temperature reaches 145°F, about 15 minutes. Tent lightly with foil for at least 5 minutes before slicing.

**Nutritional Content:**

- Calories: 158
- Fats: 6g
- Cholesterol: 74mg
- Sodium: 181mg
- Carbohydrates: 1g
- Fiber: 0g
- Protein: 24g

# Chipotle Chili

Serves 6 (2 cups per serving)
Hands-on time:20 min
Total time: 30 min

**Ingredients:**

- 1 tablespoon canola or sunflower oil
- 2 onions, chopped
- 1 pound extra-lean (7% fat) ground beef
- 2 tablespoons chili powder
- 1 tablespoon Salt-Free Southwest Seasoning Mix or Mrs. Dash, plus more if needed
- 1/2 teaspoon salt, divided
- 1 (28-ounce) can no-salt-added whole tomatoes
- 1 (5.5-ounce) can tomato paste
- 2 (15-ounce) cans no-salt-added beans of your choice, rinsed and drained
- 2 red bell peppers, seeded and chopped
- 2 medium zucchini, cut into bite-size pieces
- 1 tablespoon pure maple syrup

**Method:**

1. In a large pot, heat the oil. Add the beef and onions, and cook over medium-high heat, stirring to brown evenly, 7 to 10 minutes.
2. Add the chili powder, Southwest seasoning, and 1/4 teaspoon of salt and stir for 1 minute. Add the tomatoes with their juice, tomato paste, beans, bell peppers, zucchini, and maple syrup. Turn up the heat to bring it to a boil, then turn it down to medium-low and simmer for 10 minutes.
3. Taste, and add another 1/4 teaspoon of salt or more Southwest Seasoning, if desired.

**Nutritional Content:**

- Calories: 347
- Fats: 9g
- Cholesterol: 48mg
- Sodium: 365mg
- Carbohydrates: 41g
- Fiber: 14g
- Protein: 27g

# Grilled Tip Sirloin Steak With Mango Salsa

Dairy-free, gluten-free, quick & easy
Prep time: 5 minutes
Cook time: 15 minutes

## Ingredients:

- 2 (4-ounce) sirloin steaks
- 1/8 teaspoon salt, plus more for seasoning
- 1/2 teaspoon freshly ground black pepper, plus more for seasoning
- Nonstick olive oil cooking spray
- 1 red bell pepper, sliced
- 1 mango, halved, peeled, and seeded
- 1/2 white onion, sliced
- 1 tomato, halved
- 1 tablespoon freshly squeezed lime juice
- 1/2 teaspoon apple cider vinegar
- 1/4 cup chopped fresh cilantro

## Method:

1. Prepare a grill for direct-heat cooking over hot charcoal (high heat for gas).
2. Pat the steaks dry and season them with salt and pepper.
3. Oil the grill rack and place the steak, bell pepper, mango, onion, and tomato on the grill.
4. Grill the vegetables and mango for 2 to 3 minutes. Transfer to a cutting board and dice. Place in a small bowl.
5. Turn the steaks occasionally and grill for 6 to 8 minutes for medium (140°F) or 8 to 10 minutes for medium-well (150°F) Transfer the steaks to two serving plates to rest.
6. Meanwhile, stir the lime juice, vinegar, and cilantro into the grilled mango mixture.
7. Season the salsa with 1/8 teaspoon of salt and 1/2 teaspoon of pepper and serve over the steaks.

## Nutritional Content:

- Calories: 349
- Fats: 8g
- Protein: 37g
- Cholesterol: 101mg
- Carbohydrates: 34g
- Fiber: 5g
- Sodium: 229mg

# Alberta Steak Salad With Roasted Baby Potatoes

Serves 4
Hands-on time: 30 min
Total time: 30 min

**Ingredients:**

- 1½ pounds small new potatoes
- 2 tablespoons canola or sunflower oil, divided
- 1/2 teaspoon kosher salt, divided
- Freshly ground black pepper
- 1 pound beef tenderloin steaks, trimmed of visible fat
- 1 head butter lettuce, torn into pieces
- 1/2 cup no-salt-added canned chickpeas, rinsed and drained
- 1 baby cucumber, sliced
- 1 medium carrot, peeled and shredded or spiralized
- 1/2 cup Red Wine Vinaigrette
- 1 medium beet, peeled and shredded or spiralized

**Method:**

1. Preheat the oven to 400°F.
2. Spread the potatoes on a rimmed baking sheet. Add 1 tablespoon of oil, 1/4 teaspoon of salt, and pepper. Toss well, and slide the baking sheet into the oven; roast the potatoes for 30 minutes.
3. Meanwhile, pat the steaks dry with a paper towel, and season with the remaining 1/4 teaspoon of salt and pepper. Heat the remaining 1 tablespoon of oil in an oven-safe skillet over medium-high heat. When the skillet is very hot, cook the steaks until they are browned to your liking, 2 to 3 minutes per side. (Reduce the heat if the steaks are burning.) Put the skillet with the steaks in the oven, and roast to your desired level of doneness, 7 to 10 minutes. (A meat thermometer should read between 120°F for rare to 145°F for medium-well done. The temperature will continue to rise while the meat rests.)
4. While the meat and potatoes are cooking, combine the lettuce, chickpeas, cucumber, and carrot in a large bowl.
5. When the steak is ready, transfer it to a cutting board and tent with aluminum foil. Let it rest for at least 5 minutes before slicing against the grain.
6. Toss the salad with the vinaigrette, and top with the steak and beets. Serve the potatoes on the side.

**Nutritional Content:**

- Calories: 536
- Fats: 28g
- Cholesterol: 69mg
- Sodium: 474mg

- Carbohydrates: 42g
- Fiber: 7g
- Protein: 31g

# Pork Chops With Mushroom Gravy

Serves 4
Hands-on time: 15 min
Total time: 15 min

**Ingredients:**

- 1 recipe Mushroom and Thyme Gravy
- 1 tablespoon canola or sunflower oil
- 4 bone-in pork loin chops
- 1/4 teaspoon kosher salt
- Freshly ground black pepper
- 1 (11-ounce) package baby spinach or 2 bunches spinach, torn into bite-size pieces

**Method:**

1. In a small saucepan, bring the gravy to a simmer over low heat.
2. Heat the oil in a large, heavy skillet over medium-high heat. Pat the pork chops dry, and season both sides with salt and pepper. When the oil is hot, add the pork chops and cook without touching for 3 to 4 minutes on each side, until the pork reaches an internal temperature of 145°F. The meat should be pale and white with mostly clear juices. Transfer the pork chops to a plate, and tent with aluminum foil.
3. Turn the heat down, and add the spinach and a splash of water to the pan. Cook for 1 to 2 minutes, until the spinach is wilted.
4. Serve the pork on a bed of spinach, topped with the gravy.

**Nutritional Content:**

- Calories: 326
- Fats: 20g
- Cholesterol: 74mg
- Sodium: 485mg
- Carbohydrates: 10g
- Fiber: 3g
- Protein: 27g

# Pan-Seared Pork Medallions With Pears

Serves 4
Hands-on time: 25 min
Total time: 30 min

## Ingredients:

- 2 cups water
- 1 cup uncooked pearl barley
- 1 (1-pound) boneless pork tenderloin roast
- 1/2 teaspoon kosher salt
- Freshly ground black pepper
- 1 tablespoon canola or sunflower oil
- 3 celery stalks, chopped
- 2 shallots, chopped
- 1 garlic clove, minced
- 1 tablespoon unsalted butter
- 1/2 teaspoon dried rosemary
- 1/4 teaspoon ground ginger
- 1 tablespoon all-purpose flour
- 1 cup reduced-sodium chicken broth
- 1 (15-ounce) can sliced pears, drained

## Method:

1. Bring the water to a boil in a large pot over high heat. Add the barley. Cover the pot, reduce the heat, and simmer for 25 minutes or until tender.
2. Meanwhile, trim the tenderloin of any silverskin, and pat it dry. Slice the tenderloin into 1/2-inch-thick medallions. Sprinkle with salt and pepper.
3. Heat the oil in a large skillet over medium-high heat. When it is hot, cook the pork until it is browned on both sides, about 3 minutes per side. Transfer to a plate, and tent with aluminum foil.
4. Add the celery, shallots, garlic, butter, rosemary, and ginger to the skillet, and sauté for 2 to 3 minutes. Stir in the flour until blended. Then gradually add the broth, stirring constantly, until the mixture comes to a boil. Cook and stir for 1 minute, until thickened.
5. Add the pears, and return the pork to the skillet. Taste and adjust the seasoning, if needed. Serve the pork, pears, and sauce over the barley.

## Nutritional Content:

- Calories: 438
- Fats: 10g
- Cholesterol: 82mg
- Sodium: 362mg

- Carbohydrates: 58g
- Fiber: 10g
- Protein: 30g

# Chapter 8: Snacks and Sides

## Garlicky Kale Chips

Serves 4
Hands-on time: 5 min
Total time: 25 min

**Ingredients:**

- 1 bunch curly kale
- 2 teaspoons extra-virgin olive oil
- 1/4 teaspoon kosher salt
- 1/4 teaspoon garlic powder (optional)

**Method:**

1. Preheat the oven to 325°F. Line a rimmed baking sheet with parchment paper.
2. Remove the tough stems from the kale, and tear the leaves into squares about the size of big potato chips (they'll shrink when cooked).
3. Transfer the kale to a large bowl, and drizzle with the oil. Massage with your fingers for 1 to 2 minutes to coat well. Spread out on the baking sheet.
4. Cook for 8 minutes, then toss and cook for another 7 minutes and check them. Take them out as soon as they feel crispy, likely within the next 5 minutes.
5. Sprinkle with salt and garlic powder (if using). Enjoy immediately.

**Nutritional Content:**

- Calories: 28
- Fats: 2g
- Cholesterol: 0mg
- Sodium: 126mg
- Carbohydrates: 2g
- Fiber: 1g
- Protein: 1g

# Roasted Brussels Sprouts

Dairy-free, gluten-free, vegan, quick & easy
Prep time: 5 minutes
Cook time: 12 minutes

## Ingredients:

- 1 cup Brussels sprouts
- 1 teaspoon olive oil
- 1 teaspoon balsamic vinegar
- Salt
- Freshly ground black pepper

## Method:

1. Preheat the oven to 450°F and line a baking sheet with aluminum foil.
2. Trim the ends of the Brussels sprouts and remove any bruised outer leaves. Halve the sprouts and place them on the prepared baking sheet. Add the olive oil and vinegar and season with salt and pepper. Using your hands, mix them together to coat. Spread the sprouts out in a single layer, being careful not to overcrowd them.
3. Bake for 10 to 12 minutes, stirring them halfway through. Serve warm.

## Nutritional Content:

- Calories: 40
- Fats: 3g
- Protein: 2g
- Cholesterol: 0mg
- Carbohydrates: 4g
- Fiber: 2g
- Sodium: 89mg

# Oven-Roasted Sweet Potato Fries

Dairy-free, gluten-free, vegan
Prep time: 5 minutes
Cook time: 30 minutes

## Ingredients:

- 2 sweet potatoes, scrubbed
- 1 tablespoon olive oil
- 1 teaspoon garlic powder
- 1 teaspoon paprika
- 1/4 teaspoon freshly ground black pepper
- 1/8 teaspoon cayenne pepper
- 1/8 teaspoon salt

## Method:

1. Preheat the oven to 425°F
2. Leaving the skins on and using a very sharp knife, cut the sweet potatoes into thin, even matchsticks.
3. Transfer the matchsticks to a large baking sheet and drizzle with the olive oil. Sprinkle with the garlic powder, paprika, black pepper, cayenne pepper, and salt and toss to coat. Arrange the potatoes in a single layer to ensure they crisp up.
4. Bake for 15 minutes and flip to cook the other side. Bake for an additional 10 to 15 minutes, or until crispy and brown. Serve immediately.

## Nutritional Content:

- Calories: 334
- Fats: 8g
- Protein: 4g
- Cholesterol: 0mg
- Carbohydrates: 65g
- Fiber: 10g
- Sodium: 168mg

# Baked Tortilla Chips

Serves 4
Hands-on time: 5 min
Total time: 20 min

**Ingredients:**

- 1 tablespoon canola or sunflower oil
- 4 medium whole-wheat tortillas
- 1/8 teaspoon coarse salt

**Method:**

1. Preheat the oven to 350°F.
2. Brush the oil onto both sides of each tortilla. Stack them on a large cutting board, and cut the entire stack at once, cutting the stack into 8 wedges of each tortilla. Transfer the tortilla pieces to a rimmed baking sheet. Sprinkle a little salt over each chip.
3. Bake for 10 minutes, and then flip the chips. Bake for another 3 to 5 minutes, until they're just starting to brown.

**Nutritional Content:**

- Calories: 192
- Fats: 11g
- Cholesterol: 0mg
- Sodium: 347mg
- Carbohydrates: 20g
- Fiber: 4g
- Protein: 4g

# Sesame-Garlic Edamame

Serves 4
Hands-on time: 10 min
Total time: 10 min

## Ingredients:

- 1 (14-ounce) package frozen edamame in their shells
- 1 tablespoon canola or sunflower oil
- 1 tablespoon toasted sesame oil
- 3 garlic cloves, minced
- 1/2 teaspoon kosher salt
- 1/4 teaspoon red pepper flakes (or more)

## Method:

1. Bring a large pot of water to a boil over high heat. Add the edamame, and cook just long enough to warm them up, 2 to 3 minutes.
2. Meanwhile, heat the canola oil, sesame oil, garlic, salt, and red pepper flakes in a large skillet over medium heat for 1 to 2 minutes, then remove the pan from the heat.
3. Drain the edamame and add them to the skillet, tossing to combine.

## Nutritional Content:

- Calories: 173
- Fats: 12g
- Cholesterol: 0mg
- Sodium: 246mg
- Carbohydrates: 8g
- Fiber: 5g
- Protein: 11g

# Spicy Guacamole

Serves 4 (about 3 tablespoons per serving)
Hands-on time: 15 min
Total time: 15 min

**Ingredients:**

- 1 ripe avocado, peeled, pitted, and mashed
- 1½ tablespoons freshly squeezed lime juice
- 1 tablespoon minced jalapeño pepper, or to taste
- 1 tablespoon minced red onion
- 1 tablespoon chopped fresh cilantro
- 1 garlic clove, minced
- 1/8 to 1/4 teaspoon kosher salt
- Freshly ground black pepper

**Method:**

1. Combine the avocado, lime juice, jalapeño, onion, cilantro, garlic, salt, and pepper in a large bowl, and mix well.

**Nutritional Content:**

- Calories: 61
- Fats: 5g
- Cholesterol: 0mg
- Sodium: 123mg
- Carbohydrates: 4g
- Fiber: 2g
- Protein: 1g

# Homemade Hash Browns

Dairy-free, gluten-free, vegan, quick & easy
Prep time: 10 minutes
Cook time: 20 minutes

## Ingredients:

- 1 sweet potato, peeled and grated
- 1 Yukon gold potato, peeled and grated
- 1/2 cup chopped spinach leaves
- 1/4 cup finely chopped onion
- 1/4 cup grated carrots
- 1/8 teaspoon salt
- 1½ tablespoons gluten-free oat flour
- Pinch freshly ground black pepper
- 2 teaspoons olive oil

## Method:

1. In a medium bowl, mix together the sweet potato, gold potato, spinach, onion, and carrots. Add the salt and mix well.
2. Using your hands, squeeze the veggie mixture to remove all the moisture. Sprinkle in the oat flour and a pinch of pepper and mix to combine. Divide the potato mixture into four mounds and form each mound into patties.
3. Heat the olive oil in a large skillet over medium-high heat. Add the patties, press down gently, and brown for 4 to 5 minutes. Decrease the heat to medium and cook for 5 minutes more. Flip the patties and continue to cook 5 to 10 more minutes, or until crispy and brown. Serve warm.

## Nutritional Content:

- Calories: 226
- Fats: 5g
- Protein: 5g
- Cholesterol: 0mg
- Carbohydrates: 42g
- Fiber: 6g
- Sodium: 204mg

# Rosemary And White Bean Dip

Serves 10(1/4cup per serving)
Hands-on time: 10 min
Total time: 10 min

**Ingredients:**

- 1 (15-ounce) can cannellini beans, rinsed and drained
- 2 tablespoons extra-virgin olive oil
- 1 garlic clove, peeled
- 1 teaspoon finely chopped fresh rosemary
- Pinch cayenne pepper
- Freshly ground black pepper
- 1 (7.5-ounce) jar marinated artichoke hearts, drained

**Method:**

1. Blend the beans, oil, garlic, rosemary, cayenne pepper, and black pepper in a food processor until smooth.
2. Add the artichoke hearts, and pulse until roughly chopped but not puréed.

**Nutritional Content:**

- Calories: 75
- Fats: 5g
- Cholesterol: 0mg
- Sodium: 139mg
- Carbohydrates: 6g
- Fiber: 3g
- Protein: 2g

# Cauliflower Mashed "Potatoes"

Gluten-free, quick & easy
Prep time: 5 minutes
Cook time: 8 minutes

## Ingredients:

- 1½-pound head of cauliflower, chopped into florets
- 3 garlic cloves, chopped
- 1 teaspoon fresh thyme
- 1 teaspoon chopped fresh chives
- 1 teaspoon olive oil
- 2 tablespoons nonfat milk or plant-based mill
- Pinch salt
- Pinch freshly ground black pepper

## Method:

1. Fill a large saucepan with about 1 inch of water and insert a steamer basket. Bring the water to a boil and add the cauliflower florets to the basket. Decrease the heat to a simmer and cover, allowing the cauliflower to steam for 6 to 8 minutes, or until fork-tender.
2. Drain the steamed cauliflower and transfer it to the bowl of a large food processor. Add the garlic, thyme, chives, olive oil, milk, salt, and pepper, and process to your desired texture. Serve warm.

## Nutritional Content:

- Calories: 119
- Fats: 3g
- Protein: 8g
- Cholesterol: 0mg
- Carbohydrates: 21g
- Fiber: 9g
- Sodium: 189mg

# Oven-Roasted Garlic Cabbage

Dairy-free, gluten-free, vegan
Prep time: 5 minutes
Cook time: 40 minutes

## Ingredients:

- 1/2 head of cabbage, cut into 1-inch-thick slices
- 1 tablespoon olive oil
- 3 garlic cloves, minced
- 1 tablespoon dried chives
- Salt
- Freshly ground black pepper

## Method:

1. Preheat the oven to 400°F.
2. Brush both sides of the cabbage slices with the olive oil.
3. Pat the garlic evenly onto each side of the cabbage slices. Sprinkle each side with chives then season them with salt and pepper. Lay the slices on a baking sheet.
4. Roast for 20 minutes, turn the slices over, and roast for another 20 minutes, or until the edges are crispy. Serve immediately.

## Nutritional Content:

- Calories: 117
- Fats: 7g
- Protein: 3g
- Cholesterol: 0mg
- Carbohydrates: 13g
- Fiber: 5g
- Sodium: 114mg

# Chapter 9: Desserts

## Pumpkin Cakes

Dairy-free, gluten-free, vegan
Prep time: 10 minutes
Cook time: 25 minutes

### Ingredients:

- 1/4 cup canned pumpkin purée
- 1 tablespoon unsweetened almond milk or nonfat milk
- 1 tablespoon dark brown sugar
- 1 tablespoon granulated sugar
- 1 tablespoon olive oil
- 1/2 teaspoon pumpkin pie spice, plus more for garnish
- 1/4 cup gluten-free oat flour
- 1/2 teaspoon baking powder
- 1/8 teaspoon salt

### Method:

1. Preheat the oven to 350°F.
2. In a small bowl, whisk together the pumpkin purée, almond milk, brown sugar, granulated sugar, olive oil, and pumpkin pie spice.
3. Fold in the flour, baking powder, and salt.
4. Divide the mixture evenly between two 4- ounce ramekins and bake for 24 to 26 minutes, or until a toothpick inserted in the center comes out clean.
5. Serve with an extra dusting of pumpkin pie spice.

### Nutritional Content:

- Calories: 159
- Fats: 8g
- Protein: 2g
- Cholesterol: 0mg
- Carbohydrates: 22g
- Fiber: 2g
- Sodium: 155mg

# Chocolate-Cashew Spread

Makes 1/2 cup (2 tablespoons per serving)
Hands-on time: 10 min
Total time: 10 min

## Ingredients:

- 1/4 cup unsalted cashew butter
- 3 tablespoons water
- 1½ tablespoons unsweetened cocoa powder
- 2 teaspoons honey
- 1 teaspoon extra-virgin olive oil
- 1/2 teaspoon vanilla extract
- Pinch of ground cinnamon
- Pinch of salt

## Method:

1. Stir together the cashew butter, water, cocoa powder, honey, olive oil, vanilla, cinnamon, and salt in a large bowl until smooth, 2 to 3 minutes.

## Nutritional Content:

- Calories: 108
- Fats: 9g
- Cholesterol: 0mg
- Sodium: 93mg
- Carbohydrates: 8g
- Fiber: 1g
- Protein: 2g

# Chocolate Cherry "Ice Cream"

Dairy-free, gluten-free
Prep time: 5 minutes, plus 1 hour chilling time

**Ingredients:**

- 1/2 avocado, peeled and seeded
- 1½ cups frozen cherries
- 2 teaspoons honey
- 1 pitted date, chopped
- 1 tablespoon unsweetened cocoa powder
- 5 tablespoons unsweetened almond milk, plus more as
- needed, or nonfat milk
- 1 teaspoon vanilla extract
- Pinch salt
- Pinch stevia (optional)

**Method:**

1. Add all the ingredients to a food processor and process, scraping down the sides occasionally, for 3 to 5 minutes, or until smooth and the consistency of ice cream.
2. Scoop into a bowl and enjoy immediately or, for a firmer ice cream, transfer to an airtight freezer-safe container and freeze for at least 1 hour.

**Nutritional Content:**

- Calories: 215
- Fats: 11g
- Protein: 4g
- Cholesterol: 1mg
- Carbohydrates: 30g
- Fiber: 7g
- Sodium: 103mg

# Frosted Vanilla Cupcakes

Gluten-free, quick & easy
Prep time: 10 minutes
Cook time: 15 minutes

**Ingredients:**

- 1 egg white
- 1½ tablespoons brown sugar
- 1 tablespoon unsweetened applesauce
- 1 tablespoon olive oil
- 3/4 teaspoon vanilla extract
- 1/4 cup gluten-free oat flour
- 1/4 teaspoon baking powder
- Pinch salt
- 1½ tablespoons nonfat milk or plant-based milk
- 1 tablespoon nonfat cream cheese, at room temperature
- 1 teaspoon powdered sugar
- 1/2 tablespoon freshly grated lemon zest
- 1 lemon, halved
- 1/4 cup fresh blueberries, for garnish

**Method:**

1. Preheat the oven to 350°F and spray two cups of a cupcake tin with non-stick cooking spray, or line them with cupcake liners.
2. In a small bowl, whisk together the egg white and brown sugar.
3. Add the applesauce, olive oil, and vanilla and stir to combine. Stir in the flour, baking powder, and salt until combined. Stir in the milk until smooth.
4. Pour into the prepared cups and bake for 10 to 15 minutes, or until cooked through.
5. Meanwhile, stir together the cream cheese, powdered sugar, and lemon zest. Drizzle in just a touch of lemon juice and place the frosting in the refrigerator.
6. Once the cupcakes have cooled, divide the frosting between the two cupcakes, top with fresh blueberries, and serve.

**Nutritional Content:**

- Calories: 185
- Fats: 6g
- Protein: 4g
- Cholesterol: 6mg
- Carbohydrates: 21g
- Fiber: 2g
- Sodium: 118mg

# Grano Dolce Light (Sweet Wheat)

Serves 6
Hands-on time: 20 min
Total time: 30 min

## Ingredients:

- 2/3 cup uncooked farro
- 1/8 teaspoon salt
- 1/4 cup walnuts
- 1/4 cup almonds
- 1 pomegranate
- 2 tablespoons plus 1 teaspoon honey, divided
- 1/2 cup 5% plain Greek yogurt
- 1 teaspoon apple cider vinegar
- 1/4 teaspoon ground cinnamon
- 2 ounces dark chocolate (70% + cacao ), cut into 1/2 -inch squares

## Method:

1. Preheat the oven to 350°F.
2. Cook the farro with the salt until tender, according to the package directions.
3. Toast the nuts on a rimmed baking sheet in the oven. Shake them after 5 minutes, check after another 3 minutes, and take them out when they look golden and smell nutty, usually after no more than 12 minutes total. Remove from the pan to cool, then chop roughly.
4. Meanwhile, release the pomegranate seeds (see Tip); set them aside.
5. Mix 1 teaspoon of honey into the yogurt in a small bowl.
6. Whisk the vinegar with the remaining 2 tablespoons of honey and the cinnamon in a large bowl. Toss this mixture with the cooked farro.
7. Let it cool to about room temperature, then toss gently with the pomegranate seeds, nuts, and chocolate. Spoon into wine glasses or small mason jars, and top with the sweetened yogurt.

## Nutritional Content:

- Calories: 274
- Fats: 12g
- Cholesterol: 3mg
- Sodium: 61mg
- Carbohydrates: 36g
- Fiber: 7g
- Protein: 8g

# Marsala-Poached Figs Over Ricotta

Gluten-Free, Quick & Easy
Prep Time: 5 Minutes
Cook Time: 5 Minutes

## Ingredients:

- 1/2 cup quartered dried figs
- 1/4 cup Marsala or port
- 2 teaspoons honey
- 1/2 cup part-skim ricotta cheese
- 1/2 teaspoon granulated stevia, or 1 teaspoon sugar
- 1/4 teaspoon vanilla extract
- 1½ tablespoons toasted slivered almonds

## Method:

1. Place the figs, Marsala, and honey in a small saucepan. Bring to a boil, decrease the heat, and simmer for 5 minutes, or until the figs soften and the wine is syrupy.
2. Meanwhile, in a small bowl, stir together the ricotta, stevia, and vanilla. Divide between two bowls, top with the fig mixture and the almonds, and serve.

## Nutritional Content:

- Calories: 290
- Fats: 8g
- Protein: 10g
- Cholesterol: 19mg
- Carbohydrates: 45g
- Fiber: 5g
- Sodium: 84mg

# Berries with Greek Yogurt Dressing

Gluten-free, quick & easy
Prep time: 5 minutes

## Ingredients:

- 2 cups mixed berries (raspberries, blueberries, cherries)
- 1 cup plain nonfat Greek yogurt
- 1/4 cup honey
- 1/2 teaspoon vanilla extract
- Pinch ground cinnamon

## Method:

1. Wash the berries in a colander and portion into two serving dishes.
2. In a small bowl, combine the Greek yogurt, honey, vanilla, and cinnamon and whisk until fully combined.
3. Top each dish of berries with half of the yogurt dressing.
4. Enjoy immediately.

## Nutritional Content:

- Calories: 283
- Fats: 2g
- Protein: 9g
- Cholesterol: 7mg
- Carbohydrates: 59g
- Fiber: 8g
- Sodium: 89mg

# Banana-Oatmeal Cookies

Makes 30 medium cookies (1 per serving)
Hands-on time: 15 min
Total time: 30 min

**Ingredients:**

- 1/2 cup Better Butter or 1/4 cup unsalted butter plus 1/4cup canola or sunflower oil
- 1 cup packed brown sugar
- 1 large egg
- 2 large, ripe bananas, mashed
- 2 teaspoons vanilla extract
- 1/2 cup all-purpose flour
- 1/2 cup whole-wheat flour
- 1 teaspoon salt
- 1/2 teaspoon baking soda
- 3 cups rolled oats

**Method:**

1. Preheat the oven to 375°F. Lightly oil two rimmed baking sheets.
2. Cream the Better Butter, brown sugar, and egg in a large bowl. Stir in the mashed bananas and vanilla.
3. In another medium bowl, combine the flours, salt, and baking soda. Add to the banana mixture. Mix in the oats.
4. Drop tablespoon-size rounds onto the baking sheets. Bake for 12 to 13 minutes, watching closely near the end so the cookies don't burn.

**Nutritional Content:**

- Calories: 118
- Fats: 4g
- Cholesterol: 10mg
- Sodium: 104mg
- Carbohydrates: 18g
- Fiber: 2g
- Protein: 2g

# Dark Chocolate Avocado Mousse

Gluten-free
Prep time: 10 minutes,
Plus 1 hour chilling time

**Ingredients:**

- 1 large very ripe avocado, peeled and seeded
- 2 ounces 70%cacao baking chocolate, melted
- 2 tablespoons unsweetened cocoa powder
- 1/4 cup unsweetened almond milk or nonfat milk
- 2 tablespoons maple syrup
- 1/4 teaspoon vanilla extract
- Pinch ground cinnamon
- Pinch salt

**Method:**

1. In a food processor, combine the avocado, melted chocolate, cocoa powder, almond milk, maple syrup, vanilla, cinnamon, and salt and process until smooth. Use less milk for a thicker mousse and more for a thinner consistency.
2. Spoon the mousse into two small ramekins and chill in the refrigerator for at least 1 hour before serving.

**Nutritional Content:**

- Calories: 434
- Fats: 29g
- Protein: 6g
- Cholesterol: 7mg
- Carbohydrates: 53g
- Fiber: 9g
- Sodium: 125mg

# Dark Hot Chocolate

Serves 2
Hands-on time: 5 min
Total time: 5 min

**Ingredients:**

- 1¾ cups vanilla soy milk
- 1 ounce dark chocolate (70% cacao or more), broken into small pieces

**Method:**

1. Heat the soy milk in a small saucepan over medium-high heat and add the chocolate. When the milk starts bubbling, turn the heat to low.
2. Whisk until the chocolate is melted and fully incorporated. Tip the pot to make sure there is no remaining chocolate on the bottom.

**Nutritional Content:**

- Calories: 149
- Fats: 8g
- Cholesterol: 0mg
- Sodium: 105mg
- Carbohydrates: 14g
- Fiber: 2g
- Protein: 6g

# Broiled Mango

Dairy-free, gluten-free, vegan, quick & easy
Prep time: 5 minutes
Cook time: 10 minutes

## Ingredients:

- 1 mango, peeled, seeded, and sliced
- 1 lime, cut into wedges

## Method:

1. Position the rack in the upper third of the oven and preheat the broiler. Line a broiler pan with aluminum foil.
2. Arrange the mango slices in a single layer in the prepared pan. Broil for 8 to 10 minutes, or until browned in spots. Transfer to two plates, squeeze lime wedges over the broiled mango, and serve.

## Nutritional Content:

- Calories: 101
- Fats: 1g
- Protein: 1g
- Cholesterol: 0mg
- Carbohydrates: 25g
- Fiber: 3g
- Sodium: 2mg

# Stovetop Apple Crisp

Serves 4
Hands-on time: 15 min
Total time: 20 min

**Ingredients:**

- 1 pound red apples, cored and sliced (about 5)
- 1/3 cup water
- 1 teaspoon plus 1 tablespoon packed brown sugar, divided
- 1/4 teaspoon freshly squeezed lemon juice (optional)
- 1/4 cup rolled oats
- 1/4 cup chopped walnuts
- 1 tablespoon unsalted butter
- 1/4 teaspoon ground cinnamon
- Pinch salt
- 2 tablespoons dried cranberries (optional)

**Method:**

1. Put the apples and water in a large pot or sauté pan, and bring to a boil over medium-high heat. When the water starts to boil, turn the heat down to medium-low, cover, and cook for 5 to 10 minutes. Check it and stir every few minutes, adding more water if needed.
2. When the apples are just about soft enough for your liking, take the lid off and cook until any excess liquid has evaporated. Taste an apple; add 1 teaspoon of brown sugar if they're too tart, or add the lemon juice if they're too sweet. (The cooking time and additions needed will vary by type of apple and personal preference.)
3. Meanwhile, combine the oats, walnuts, butter, cinnamon, salt, and 1 tablespoon of brown sugar in a small skillet. Cook over medium heat, stirring occasionally, until everything is toasty and fragrant.
4. Top the stewed apples with the crispy nuts and oats, as well as a sprinkle of dried cranberries, if you like.

**Nutritional Content:**

- Calories: 185
- Fats: 8g
- Cholesterol: 8mg
- Sodium: 42mg
- Carbohydrates: 299g
- Fiber: 4g
- Protein: 2g

# Almond Butter And Banana Wrap

Serves 1
Hands-on time:5 min
Total time: 5 min

## Ingredients:

- 2 tablespoons natural almond butter
- 1 whole-wheat tortilla
- 1 banana

## Method:

1. Spread the almond butter on the tortilla.
2. Place the banana across the middle of the tortilla, and wrap it up. Cut into three pieces, if you like.

## Nutritional Content:

- Calories: 433
- Fats: 22g
- Cholesterol: 0mg
- Sodium: 361mg

- Carbohydrates: 52g
- Fiber: 11g
- Protein: 12g

# Mango Chiller

Serves 4(1/2 cup per serving)
Hands-on time: 5 min
Total time: 5 min

## Ingredients:

- 2 cups frozen mango chunks
- 1/2 cup plain 2% Greek yogurt
- 1/4 cup 1% milk
- 2 teaspoons honey (optional)

## Method:

1. Mix the mango and yogurt in a food processor or blender. Add the milk, a bit at a time, to get it to the consistency of soft ice cream.
2. Taste, and add honey if you like. Enjoy immediately.

## Nutritional Content:

- Calories: 85
- Fats: 1g
- Cholesterol: 4mg
- Sodium: 17mg
- Carbohydrates: 16g
- Fiber: 1g
- Protein: 4g

# Blueberry-Ricotta Swirl

Serves 2
Hands-on time: 5 min
Total time: 5 min

## Ingredients:

- 1/2 cup fresh or frozen blueberries
- 1/2 cup part-skim ricotta cheese
- 1 teaspoon sugar
- 1/2 teaspoon lemon zest (optional)

## Method:

1. If using frozen blueberries, warm them in a saucepan over medium heat until they are thawed but not hot.
2. Meanwhile, mix the sugar with the ricotta in a medium bowl.
3. Mix the blueberries into the ricotta, leaving a few out. Taste, and add more sugar if desired. Top with the remaining blueberries and lemon zest (if using).

## Nutritional Content:

- Calories: 113
- Fats: 5g
- Cholesterol: 19mg
- Sodium: 62mg
- Carbohydrates: 10g
- Fiber: 1g
- Protein: 7g

# Chapter 10: Staples

## Lemon-Tahini Dressing

Makes 3/4 cup (2 tablespoons per serving)
Hands-on time: 5 min
Total time: 5 min

### Ingredients:

- 1/3 cup extra-virgin olive oil
- 2 tablespoons nutritional yeast
- 2 tablespoons freshly squeezed lemon juice
- 2 tablespoons water
- 1 tablespoon reduced-sodium tamari
- 1 tablespoon tahini
- 1 small garlic clove, minced

### Method:

1. Mix the olive oil, nutritional yeast, lemon juice, water, tamari, tahini, and garlic in a mini-food processor, or whisk the ingredients by hand in a large bowl.
2. Store in an airtight container in the refrigerator for up to 1 week.

### Nutritional Content:

- Calories: 132
- Fats: 14g
- Cholesterol: 0mg
- Sodium: 122mg
- Carbohydrates: 2g
- Fiber: 0g
- Protein: 1g

# Salt-Free Southwest Seasoning Mix

Makes 1/4 cup (1 teaspoon per serving)
Hands-on time: 5 min
Total time: 5 min

## Ingredients:

- 2 tablespoons chili powder
- 2 teaspoons garlic powder
- 2 teaspoons onion powder
- 1 teaspoon chipotle powder
- 1 teaspoon dried oregano
- 1 teaspoon dried thyme

## Method:

1. Mix the chili powder, garlic powder, onion powder, chipotle powder, oregano, and thyme together in a small bowl.
2. Store in an airtight container.

## Nutritional Content:

- Calories: 11
- Fats: 0g
- Cholesterol: 0mg
- Sodium: 1mg
- Carbohydrates: 3g
- Fiber: 0g
- Protein: 0g

# Red Wine Vinaigrette

Makes 1 cup (2 tablespoons per serving)
Hands-on time: 5 min
Total time: 5 min

## Ingredients:

- 1/2 cup extra-virgin olive oil
- 3 tablespoons red wine vinegar
- 2 tablespoons Dijon mustard
- 2 teaspoons honey
- 1 small shallot, minced (optional)
- 1/4 teaspoon salt (optional)
- 1/4 teaspoon freshly ground black pepper

## Method:

1. Combine the olive oil, vinegar, mustard, honey, shallot and salt (if using), and pepper in a mini-food processor, or whisk the ingredients by hand in a large bowl.
2. Store in an airtight container in the refrigerator for up to 1 week.

## Nutritional Content:

- Calories: 142
- Fats: 15g
- Cholesterol: 0mg
- Sodium: 153mg
- Carbohydrates: 2g
- Fiber: 0g
- Protein: 0g

# Tomato-Balsamic Vinaigrette

Makes 1 cup (1/4 cup per serving)
Hands-on time: 5 min
Total time: 5 min

## Ingredients:

- 1 medium ripe tomato, seeded and diced
- 1/2 shallot, minced
- 1/4 cup extra-virgin olive oil
- 2 tablespoons balsamic vinegar
- 1/4 teaspoon freshly ground black pepper
- 1/8 teaspoon salt

## Method:

1. Gently mix the tomato, shallot, olive oil. vinegar, pepper, and salt in a large bowl.
2. Store in an airtight container in the refrigerator for up to 1 week.

## Nutritional Content:

- Calories: 133
- Fats: 14g
- Cholesterol: 0mg
- Sodium: 76mg
- Carbohydrates: 3g
- Fiber: 0g
- Protein: 0g

# Chimichurri

Serves 4
Hands-on time: 10 min
Total time: 10 min

**Ingredients:**

- 1/4 cup extra virgin olive oil
- 2 tablespoons red wine vinegar
- 2 shallots, peeled
- 2 garlic cloves, peeled
- 1/4 cup fresh flat-leaf parsley
- 1/4 cup fresh cilantro
- 1 teaspoon dried oregano
- 1/4 teaspoon kosher salt
- Freshly ground black pepper

**Method:**

1. Combine the olive oil, vinegar, shallots, garlic, parsley, cilantro, oregano, salt, and pepper in a food processor or mini-chopper. Pulse until the herbs are minced but not puréed. If you don't have a food processor, finely chop the shallots, herbs, and garlic, and mix with the other ingredients in a medium bowl.
2. Store in an airtight container in the refrigerator for up to 1 week.

**Nutritional Content:**

- Calories: 131
- Fats: 14g
- Cholesterol: 0mg
- Sodium: 125mg
- Carbohydrates: 2g
- Fiber: 1g
- Protein: 0g

# Spaghetti Sauce

Dairy-free, gluten-free, vegan
Makes 3½ cups, serving size 1/2 cup
Prep time: 5 minutes
Cook time: 35 minutes

## Ingredients:

- Olive oil nonstick cooking spray
- 1/4 cup chopped onion
- 3 garlic cloves, minced
- 1 (15-ounce) can tomato sauce, no salt added
- 1/2 cup tomato paste, no salt added
- 1½ cups water
- 1/2 teaspoon unsweetened cocoa (optional)
- 2 tablespoons dried basil
- 2 teaspoons dried oregano
- 1/2 teaspoon red pepper flakes
- 1/8 teaspoon salt
- Freshly ground black pepper

## Method:

1. Spray a large skillet with cooking spray and heat over medium heat. Add the onion and garlic to the skillet and sauté for 4 to 5 minutes, or until fragrant and translucent.
2. Add the tomato sauce, tomato paste, and water and stir to combine.
3. Add the cocoa (if using), basil, oregano, red pepper flakes, salt, and a few grinds of pepper and simmer on low for 20 to 30 minutes. Serve over pasta, grains, or vegetables.

## Nutritional Content:

- Calories: 36
- Fats: 0g
- Protein: 2g
- Cholesterol: 0mg
- Carbohydrates: 8g
- Fiber: 2g

- Sodium: 98mg

# Better Butter

Makes about 2 cups (1 tablespoon per serving)
Hands-on time: 5 min
Total time: 5 min

## Ingredients:

- 1 cup unsalted butter, softened to room temperature
- 1¼ cups canola or sunflower oil

## Method:

1. Blend the butter and oil together in the food processor until the mixture is perfectly smooth. It may take 2 to 3 minutes.
2. Pour the mixture into a storage container with a lid. Store in the refrigerator.

## Nutritional Content:

- Calories: 121
- Fats: 14g
- Cholesterol: 14mg
- Sodium: 1mg

- Carbohydrates: 0g
- Fiber: 0g
- Protein: 0g

# Fruit-Infused Sparkling Water

Serves 2
Hands-on time: 5 min
Total time: 5 min

**Ingredients:**

- 1 (32-ounce/1 liter) bottle low-sodium club soda or sparkling
- water
- 3 orange segments, halved
- 5 raspberries, halved

**Method:**

1. In a pitcher, combine the club soda and fruit.
2. Drink right away, or prepare in advance for more intense flavor.

**Nutritional Content:**

- Calories: 6
- Fats: 0g
- Cholesterol: 0mg
- Sodium: 38mg
- Carbohydrates: 1g
- Fiber: 0g
- Protein: 0g

# Homemade Ketchup

Dairy-free, gluten-free, quick & easy
Makes 1½ cups, serving size 1 tablespoon
Prep time: 5 minutes
Cook time: 5 minutes

**Ingredients:**

- 1 (6-ounce) can tomato paste, no salt added
- 1/2 cup cider vinegar
- 2 tablespoons honey
- 1 teaspoon liquid smoke
- 2 teaspoons garlic powder
- 2 teaspoons onion powder
- 1/2 teaspoon freshly ground black pepper
- 1/2 teaspoon ground cloves
- 1/2 teaspoon ground ginger
- 1/2 teaspoon ground oregano
- 1/2 teaspoon smoked paprika
- 1 cup water

**Method:**

1. In a small bowl, whisk together the tomato paste, vinegar, honey, liquid smoke, garlic powder, onion powder, pepper, cloves, ginger, oregano, and paprika.
2. Whisk in 1/2 cup of water until fully incorporated. Add the remaining water 1 tablespoon at a time until you reach your desired consistency of ketchup.

**Nutritional Content:**

- Calories: 14
- Fats: 0g
- Protein: 0g
- Cholesterol: 0mg
- Carbohydrates: 3g
- Fiber: 0g
- Sodium: 8mg

# Avocado Salsa

Dairy-free, gluten-free, vegan, quick & easy
Makes 2½ cups, serving size 2 tablespoons
Prep time: 5 minutes

## Ingredients:

- 5 Roma tomatoes, chopped
- 3 avocados, peeled, pitted, and cubed
- 1/2 cup chopped red onion
- 4 tablespoons chopped fresh cilantro
- 2 garlic cloves, minced
- Juice of 1/2 lime
- 1/4 teaspoon salt
- 1/8 teaspoon freshly ground black pepper
- Dash sriracha sauce

## Method:

1. In a medium mixing bowl, mix together the tomatoes, avocados, red onion, cilantro, and garlic. Add the lime juice, salt, pepper, and sriracha and mix well. Serve immediately.

## Nutritional Content:

- Calories: 69
- Fats: 6g
- Protein: 1g
- Cholesterol: 0mg
- Carbohydrates: 4g
- Fiber: 3g
- Sodium: 35mg

# Conclusion

Food is a critical driver of heart health, and this heart healthy cookbook helps you take the wheel. The Heart Healthy Cookbook is full of simple, quick, and satisfying meals the whole family will love.Meal planning tips, a grocery shopping guide make it easy to prepare nutritious, low-sodium meals. Many recipes call for just simple ingredients, and all are designed for efficiency, perfect for when you' re short on time or energy.

Stop worrying—you' ll always have just the right amount on your plate with the Heart Healthy Cookbook .Thank you for buying this book.Now let's start your gourmet journey!

CPSIA information can be obtained
at www.ICGtesting.com
Printed in the USA
BVHW062300180122
626544BV00006BA/1178

9 781639 350544